Female Identities: A Study of Selected Women Characters in Shakespeare's Tragedies

Stephanie Wolf

Contents

1. Introduction

The roles female characters represent in Shakespeare's plays have often been discussed. On the one hand Shakespeare's women characters are described as "strong, attractive, intelligent and humane [...] [, who] challenge accepted patterns for women's behavior"[1], on the other hand, the dominance of patriarchy in Shakespeare's plays is mentioned: "Women's roles in Shakespeare's plays are far more limited than men's, both in size and in number, and female power is repeatedly characterized as threatening or even demonic"[2]. This study will focus on both point of views and will try to discover tendencies and developments with regard to Shakespeare's female characters. Despite of these controversial opinions, other contrasts in society during Shakespeare's time need to be taken into account. While patriarchy was a common norm in 16th and 17th century England, Queen Elizabeth I reigned from 1558 until 1603.[3] As an accepted regulation, marriage generally meant the subordination of the wife to her husband, but the Protestant Queen Elizabeth never got married and was therefore never confronted with this expected norm.[4] Therefore she could keep the absolute power over England to herself as the "Virgin Queen"[5]. With this historical context, it becomes clear that a female ruler gave reason to question the current expected role of women in Elizabethan society. Apart from political structures, also values and attitudes were divided into female and male ones. Therefore, the described effects of tragedies on the audience like "emotions and responses (compassion, remorse,

---

[1] Irene G. Dash. *Wooing, Wedding and Power: Women in Shakespeare's Plays.* New York: Columbia University Press, 1981. 1.

[2] Phyllis Rackin. *Shakespeare and Women*. Oxford: Oxford University Press, 2005. 48.

[3] Helen Hackett. *Virgin Mother, Maiden Queen.* London: Macmillan, 1995. 38; 213.

[4] Cf. Robert Valerius. *Weibliche Herrschaft im 16. Jahrhundert. Die Regentschaft Elizabeths I. zwischen Realpolitik, Querelle des femmes und Kult der Virgin Queen.* Herbolzheim: Centaurus Verlag, 2002. 1; 107;132.

[5] Carole Levin. *The Heart and Stomach of a King. Elizabeth I and the Politics of Sex and Power.* Philadelphia: University of Pennsylvania Press, 1994. 26.

pity, tears) […] were understood as feminine"[6]. The theatre in Shakespeare's times was in contrast to that a male domain respecting the actors on stage.

By taking these contrasting aspects into account, this study will deal with the following aspects. At first, the author's life is presented with regard to the information about the women he encountered. Furthermore, the study displays the general role of women in the 16th and 17th century. Then it deals with Shakespeare's theatre in relation to women. With regard to the historical context, this study focuses on the female protagonists of three tragedies that imply a remarkable illustration of women characters, who self-consciously co-determine the course of the plays and challenge the expected role of women in society during Shakespeare's time. These are Juliet in *Romeo and Juliet,* Lady Macbeth in *Macbeth* and Cleopatra in *Antony and Cleopatra.*

The reasons for selecting especially these characters for this study are the differences that these women characters show. The thirteen-year-old Juliet, who is determined to overcome society's restraints for her love, Lady Macbeth, who denies her good womanly nature in order to fulfill her husband's wish and Cleopatra, the powerful Egyptian queen, who struggles between love and political interests, are three women in completely different stages of their lives. What combines them is their love which each character reveals in a different way. Unlike the expected roles for women in Renaissance England, they determine and challenge their fortune through individual decisions and actions. Eventually, all women lose the battle against their opposing resistances. Incapable of coping with the consequences of their actions, they commit suicide.

Interestingly, Shakespeare depicts the loving women characters in his tragedies in different phases and positions of their life, while similarly his life as a

---

[6]Phyllis Rackin. "Engendering the Tragic Audience: The Case of Richard III." *Shakespeare and Gender: A History.* Ed. Deborah E. Barker and Ivo Kamps. London: Verso, 1995. 266.

4

playwright proceeds as well. *Romeo and Juliet* was supposedly written in 1595[7], *Macbeth* in 1605/1606[8] and *Antony and Cleopatra* in 1607[9]. But while young Shakespeare emphasizes the incalculability of fate as one reason for Juliet's (and Romeo's) downfall, he displays Lady Macbeth implicitly as a character who eventually reflects about her actions. Fate or supernatural powers do not seem to influence the experienced Cleopatra at all, for she accepts her fortune with responsibility for her own actions. Shakespeare's changing perspective regarding the depiction of his female characters is striking. A further comparison of the three women characters is likely to reveal more about the different depiction of women in the tragedies of the famous William Shakespeare.

2. Shakespeare and Women

2.1 Biography of William Shakespeare

In general, details of William Shakespeare's life are fairly unknown. For the reason that not one handwritten line of his personal documents could be found, the known biography of Shakespeare is based on formal dates. Any further information is merely speculative. William Shakespeare was baptized on 26 April 1564 in Stratford-upon-Avon's local church which leads to the assumption that he was born on the 21st, 22nd or 23rd of April that year.[10] His mother, Mary Shakespeare, born Arden, "was the daughter of a substantial local farmer"[11] and therefore belonged to a socially respected family. By the time of William

---

[7] Cf. Brian Gibbons. Introduction. William Shakespeare. *Romeo and Juliet. The Arden Shakespeare*. Ed. Gibbons. Gen. Ed. Richard Proudfoot, Ann Thompson and Scott Kastan. London: Arden Shakespeare, 1980. 26-31.

[8] Cf. Kenneth Muir. Introduction. William Shakespeare. *Macbeth. The Arden Shakespeare*. Ed. Muir. Gen. Ed. Richard Proudfoot, Ann Thompson and David Scott Kastan. London: Routledge, 1984. 15-25.

[9] Cf. John Wilders. Introduction. William Shakespeare, *Antony and Cleopatra. The Arden Shakespeare*. Ed. Wilders. Gen. Ed. Richard Proudfoot, Ann Thompson and David Scott Kastan. London: Arden Shakespeare, 1995. 69-75.

[10] Cf. Samuel Schoenbaum. *William Shakespeare: A Compact Documentary Life*. Oxford: Oxford University Press, 1987. 11-12; 24-26.

[11] Rackin, *Shakespeare and Women* 37.

Shakespeare's birth, she had already inherited parts of her father's property and next to being a housewife, she

> "was an active participant in the economic life of the household. Some of this participation can be documented from legal records concerning the sale and conveyance of various pieces or property and litigation about it in which Mary's name appears along with her husband's."[12]

Shakespeare's father, John, worked as a "glover and whittawer, or dresser of whitleather"[13]. He also became a respected man in Stratford: In 1559 he was elected principal burgess, in 1565 alderman, and could therefore wear the title "Master".[14] William Shakespeare received his formal education from attending the Stratford grammar school.[15] While growing up, he presumably encountered diverse theatre performances. At least, many opportunities were given to William Shakespeare in order to witness theatrical performances.[16] With 18 years, William Shakespeare married the approximately eight years older Anne Hathaway.[17] They had three children: Susanna, who was baptized on 26 May 1583, and the twins Hamnet and Judith, who were baptized on 2 February 1585.[18] There is also hardly any information about the life of Shakespeare's wife, "[…] the baptism of her children, the meagre bequest of a second best bed in her husband's will, and her own death"[19] in 1623[20] are the only recorded documents of her life. In contrast to Shakespeare's mother, Anne Shakespeare "was absent from the legal records of

---

[12] Rackin, *Shakespeare and Women* 34.

[13] Schoenbaum 16.

[14] Cf. Schoenbaum 34-36.

[15] Cf. Paul J. C. Franssen. "The Life and Opinions of William Shakespeare, Gentleman: Biography between Fact and Fiction." *Literature as History/ History as Literature. Fact and Fiction in Medieval to Eighteenth-Century British Literature.* Ed. Sonja Fielitz. Frankfurt/ Main, Peter Lang: 2007. 72; cf. Schoenbaum 7.

[16] Cf. Rackin, *Shakespeare and Women* 41.

[17] Cf. Rackin, *Shakespeare and Women* 37; Cf. Mark W. Scott. Introduction. *Shakespeare for Students. Critical Interpretations of "As You Like It", "Hamlet", "Julius Caesar", "Macbeth", "The Merchant of Venice", "A Midsummer Night's Dream", "Othello", and "Romeo and Juliet".* Ed Scott. Detroit: Gale, 1992. 13.

[18] Cf. Schoenbaum 93- 94.

[19] Cf. Rackin, *Shakespeare and Women* 38.

[20] Cf. Scott, Introducion 14; cf. Schoenbaum 317.

all financial affairs of William"[21]. From around 1585 until 1602 no documents about Shakespeare's life, let alone about women in his life, can be found.[22] During this period, fittingly called the "Lost Years"[23], one can only tell that Shakespeare became an actor and playwright and moved to London.[24] Whether he joined a group of players who toured the country, or whether he went on his own to London however is questionable.[25] In 1595, records of a theatre performance at Court show that Shakespeare had joined the *Lord Chamberlain's Men* and was a leading member of this acting group.[26] This group, with which Shakespeare stayed until he left the stage as an actor, later on even gained royal patronage.[27] By 1598, he had become a famous playwright and at least eight of his plays had been published under his name in quartos.[28] After his great success, he presumably moved back to his wife in Stratford-upon-Avon where he spent his last years until his death in 1616.[29] His burial is listed in the register of the Holy Trinity Church on 25 April that year.[30]

2.2 The Role of Women in the 16th and 17th Century

The composition of Shakespeare's characters cannot be judged and analyzed under a modern understanding of women's role in society. In order to realize the differences and special features between Shakespeare's female characters, socially accepted patterns concerning female behavior in marriage, family and public life

---

[21] Cf. Rackin, *Shakespeare and Women* 39.

[22] Cf. Schoenbaum 95.

[23] Schoenbaum 95.

[24] Cf. Schoenbaum 135;137; 150-151; 200-202.

[25] Cf. Schoenbaum 118.

[26] Cf. Schoenbaum 183.

[27] Cf. Schoenbaum 183.

[28] Cf. Schoenbaum 188f.

[29] Cf. Schoenbaum 279.

[30] Cf. Scott 14; cf. Schoenbaum 307.

have to be taken into account. These originated mostly from the Christian dogma in the Middle Ages prescribing certain attitudes to women which were still valid and expected in Renaissance England.[31]

For the Renaissance Protestant society in England the Bible was the guide for attitudes and regulations after which one had to live by.[32] In contrast to today's understanding, the Bible was the source of ultimate truth which was not interpreted with respect to the time it was written, but had a timeless character.[33] Whereas the moral and social norms of the Renaissance society were closely linked to the Bible, so was the norm of the role of women. Therefore, the role of women will be presented with regard to the common belief in biblical universal truth in Shakespeare's time.

The Old Testament reflects the overall patriarchal society of the 16th and 17th century in England. Women are mainly described as submissive to men like a slave to their owner or a subject to the king.[34] In one of the Ten Commandments, the wife is listed next to the regular property of a man[35]. In Shakespeare's times, the general accepted norm was women's subordination to men. Two passages in the Bible were cited most by scholars during that time to prove that this order should be seen as a natural one. During Shakespeare's time, Christian scholars blamed women for the Fall of Man and interpreted it as evidence for women's weaker intellectual and moral character. For the reason that Eve was seduced by the snake and not Adam, most Christian scholars decisively believed in the words of the Old Testament saying that the man should be the woman's master (cf. 1

---

[31] Cf. Valerius 127.

[32] Cf. Valerius 127.

[33] Cf. Valerius 127f.

[34] Cf. Valerius 128.

[35] Cf. *The Holy Bible: King James Version; The New Cambridge Paragraph Bible with the Apocrypha.* Ed. David Norton. Cambridge: Cambridge University Press, 2005. 2 Moses 20:17.

Moses 3.16).[36] The second verification was seen in Genesis I, when Adam was made before Eve and Eve was made for Adam.[37] In Shakespeare's times, many intellectuals interpreted this in this respect that the woman is the man's assistant and does not come close to his excellence for she was made after him and is therefore inferior.[38] Paul concluded "[…] as the church is subject unto Christ, so let the wives be to their own husbands in everything" (Eph. 5.24) because "[…] the head of every man is Christ: and the head of the woman is the man, […]" (1 Cor. 11.3).[39]

Even certain attitudes were labeled masculine or feminine: men were expected to be active; women were regarded to be passive by nature.[40] The passiveness of women was on the one hand interpreted as the natural result of the woman's guilt of the Fall of Man.[41] On the other hand, respecting public activities of women, Paul's speech was often referred to in which he demanded: "Let your women keep silence in the churches, for it is not permitted unto them to speak; but they are commanded to be under obedience: as also saith the law" (1 Cor. 14, 34).[42] However, a forced passiveness by social structures was not taken into account. Today, it is striking that this understanding of patriarchal hierarchy dominated family, social and public life in Shakespeare's time.[43]

---

[36]Cf. Valerius 128.

[37] Cf. Valerius 129.

[38] Cf. Valerius 129; 132.

[39] Cf. Valerius 129-130.

[40] Cf. Valerius 131.

[41] Cf. Valerius 131.

[42] Cf. Valerius 129.

[43] Cf. Valerius 130.

2.2.1 Family and Marriage

The interpretations of the Fall of Man and Genesis I had real consequences for the position of married women in Shakespeare's time. [44] The dogmatic subordination of women to men increased and became more specific when women entered marriage. Besides, women were supposed to get married or to be married; a single life was out of the question.[45] The husband was legally the head of his family and his wife, as well as his children were expected to be obedient and to honor him.[46] Furthermore, the wife lost all her lawful rights and her separate identity because married couples were regarded as one person in the eyes of the law.[47] Therefore, all possessions were given to the husband "[...] unless special provisions were made to preserve it [...]"[48].[49] Thus, women went from being dependent on the support of their fathers to an even more existential dependence to their husbands. The same righteous hierarchy was valid for the annulment of marriage. Whereas men could divorce their wives for different reasons, women did not have the right to do so.[50] Moreover, women had to face severe punishment for infidelity, while men had to fear no punishment for being unfaithful unless they interfered with another man's rights.[51]

Disregarding the fact that also aristocratic women were usually in total economic dependence to their husbands,[52] marriage was for many families also

---

[44] Cf. Valerius 133ff.

[45] Cf. Rackin, *Shakespeare and Women* 19.

[46] Cf. Doris Märtin, *Shakespeares 'Fiend-like Queens': Charakterisierung, Kontext und dramatische Funktion der destruktiven Frauenfiguren in „Henry VI", „Richard III", „King Lear" und „Macbeth"*. Heidelberg: Winter, 1992. 9; Cf. Valerius 132; 134.

[47] Cf. Märtin 9; 100; Cf. Valerius 135.

[48] Rackin. *Shakespeare and Women* 7.

[49] Cf. Valerius 135.

[50] Cf. Valerius 128.

[51] Cf. Valerius 128.

[52] Cf. Valerius 135.

the means to gain status and wealth through.[53] Parents arranged marriages without consulting their children's opinion.[54] Especially aristocratic families arranged marriages with other aristocrats to bound both families and possibly gain advantages through it.[55] To marry for reasons of love was the absolute exception, particularly in aristocratic milieus.[56]

2.2.2 Public Life

Overall, women were mostly excluded from public activities.[57] Nevertheless, aristocratic women could sometimes free themselves in certain areas from the total male domination through their power over their subordinates.[58] Nevertheless, especially certain public activities, which were granted to men of lower rank, were denied to women.[59]

The only way for a woman to gain power and wealth appeared to be through heritage. When a woman turned sixteen she was of age and therefore the righteous heiress if no male successor existed.[60] Consequently, she could own and manage her given property if her husband's will did not forbid it and as long as she stayed unmarried.[61] The "Dower law" of inheritance was a secure and established right for widows.[62] It enabled them to inherit up to a half of their former husband's

---

[53] Cf. Valerius 134; cf. Rackin, *Shakespeare and Women* 37.

[54] Cf. Valerius 134.

[55] Cf. Valerius 134.

[56] Cf. Valerius 134-135.

[57] Cf. Valerius 11.

[58] Cf. Valerius 132.

[59] Cf. Valerius 132.

[60] Cf. Valerius 135.

[61] Cf. Valerius 135.

[62] Cf. Valerius 135.

property, disregarding of a remarriage.[63] Therefore, women could gain a certain economic independence. For the reason that women got married at an early age and aristocratic women's life expectancy was higher on average, some women became wealthy through the "Dower" right.[64]

To conclude, aristocratic women were most likely only as widows able to take part in political activities or to be publicly influential as the head of an aristocratic family.[65] As widows, they could, e. g., manage their own property, gain the guardianship of their children and arrange lucrative marriages for them.[66] Despite their possibilities as widows, if women remarried they were again expected to bow to their husband's will.[67]

2.2.3 Queen Elizabeth I and Philosophical Influences

During Shakespeare's time, Elizabeth I, who was pronounced Queen "[…] *of Englande, Fraunce and Irland* […]"[68] in 1558, embodied an astonishing contrast to the social status of women.[69] She stayed unmarried during her whole life and presented herself as the "Virgin Queen"[70], which, next to her most powerful position, distinguished her from the common image of the role of women.[71] Despite the public urging of Elizabeth I to marry and preferably give birth to a

---

[63] Cf. Valerius 135.

[64] Cf. Valerius 136.

[65] Cf. Valerius 137.

[66] Cf. Valerius 137.

[67] Cf. Valerius 137.

[68] J. Payne Collier, ed. *The Egerton Papers: A Collection of Public and Private Documents. Chiefly Illustrative of the Times of Elizabeth and James I, from the Original Manuscripts, the Property of the Right Hon. Lord Francis Egerton.* "Proclamation of Queen Elizabeth." London: John Bowyer Nichols, 1840. 28. Rpt. in Robert Valerius. *Weibliche Herrschaft im 16. Jahrhundert. Die Regentschaft Elisabeths I. zwischen Realpolitik, Querelle des femmes und Kult der Virgin Queen.* Herbolzheim: Centaurus Verlag, 2002. 66.

[69] Cf. Valerius 65.

[70] Valerius 125.

[71] Cf. Jürgen Klein. *Elisabeth I. und ihre Zeit.* München: Beck, 2004. 64.

male successor increased, for the reason that this had met the general role expectations, the Queen kept her absolute power to herself and never determined a successor.[72] The reign of a female ruler was therefore publicly highly discussed and new theoretical views of the status of women in general evolved.[73] As a matter of fact, a certain controversy developed on a theoretical-philosophical level concerning the role of women in society and public life.[74] The initial question was whether women were according to ancient literature to be seen as virtuous and intelligent as men, or whether the former Christian belief with respect to Genesis I and The Fall of Man proved women to be inferior to men.[75]

Humanists in the Renaissance period saw an ideal in the culture and knowledge of the ancient world and therefore referred back to the old literature written during that time.[76] Aristotle and Plato were the most admired authors of the Renaissance and with respect to the women's position in family, marriage and public life, Catholic humanists represented some of the same values which had already been stated by Greek and Roman writers.[77]

The major views concerning the role of women by Aristotle and Plato were quite differentiated. Plato represented the utopia of equality of men and women.[78] He argued that women should have the same education and the same possibilities regarding public life.[79] This might have been the reason for some humanists to rethink women's status in Elizabethan England. In contrast to that, Aristotle believed in the hierarchical structure of man and women. However, he saw

---

[72] Cf. Valerius 73; 101-107; 123.

[73] Cf. Märtin 10; cf. Valerius 122-123.

[74] Cf. Valerius 138.

[75] Cf. Valerius 138.

[76] Cf. Valerius 149.

[77] Cf. Valerius 149.

[78] Cf. Valerius 150.

[79] Cf. Valerius 150-151.

marriage not only as a necessity but as a mutual friendship in which the partners complement each other.[80] Although Aristotle mainly corresponded with the traditional role scheme of women in the 15th and 16th century at first, the thought of the wife as a complementary partner to her husband in marriage was revolutionary for the Elizabethan time.

Referring to the views of ancient Greek and Roman philosophers, humanist's most important claim was the extension of classic education of aristocratic and wealthy people.[81] In order to read the Bible or texts by ancient philosophers the ability to be fluent in the classic languages Latin and Greek was a necessity.[82] For the reason that the general idea of the humanists was that education leads the way to the general good and to the ability to recognize the true religion and become virtuous, also women were supposed to get a classic education.[83] Nevertheless, the hierarchical structure and the role of women as mothers and wives stayed untouched.[84] According to the humanists, women should be just enough educated to fulfill their duties as their husbands' companion and their children's educator.[85] Therefore, they should only be taught in the classic languages Latin and Greek.[86] Being stuck in the role schemes of that time, humanists did not create theories that could have led to a far-reaching reformation of real conditions for women.[87]

---

[80] Cf. Valerius 151-152.

[81] Cf. Valerius 153.

[82] Cf. Valerius 153.

[83] Cf. Valerius 147; 154.

[84] Cf. Valerius 154-155.

[85] Cf. Valerius 155.

[86] Cf. Valerius 154-155.

[87] Cf. Valerius 157-158.

The reformists mainly referred to texts of the Bible, the Apostles and theologians of the Middle Ages.[88] On the whole, they saw women as supposed to be subordinate to men in all areas.[89] They based their assumption on the interpretation of Genesis I: The woman is responsible for the Fall of Man and furthermore inferior for she is made after the man.[90] Education was not granted for women although a mother was expected to function as her children's educator.[91] To sum up, one could say that the reformist's ideals came closest to the beliefs in Elizabethan society's reality.[92]

Another approach focused on the ideal of aristocratic women. The English translation of the book "Il libro del Cortegiano" by B. Castiglione, published in 1561, was very successful in England and throughout Europe and gave i. a. a concrete description of ideal female behavior at court.[93] The aristocratic women's attitudes were supposed to be passive.[94] Furthermore, according to the book's advice, a woman should only have just enough education in order to fulfill her expected duties which were dancing, painting, playing an instrument and perfect conversation.[95] Through this description it seems that the woman was seen as a mere decoration to the aristocratic man.[96]

Finally, the different theories did not bring a significant change for women in Shakespeare's time. Although Queen Elizabeth I reigned, the traditional role

---

[88] Cf. Valerius 159.

[89] Cf. Valerius 159.

[90] Cf. Valerius 159.

[91] Cf. Valerius 159ff.

[92] Cf. Valerius 161-162.

[93] Cf. Valerius 162-163.

[94] Cf. Valerius 163.

[95] Cf. Valerius 162.

[96] Cf. Valerius 163.

schemes with the general male domination, which came closest to reformist's approaches, were the norm in Elizabethan society.[97] The general social roles were clearly divided; a woman was supposed to marry and to take care of the household and children whereas men were granted to take part in public life.[98] Elizabeth I presented herself as an exception from this norm and secured her position in proclaiming she was chosen by God to be the Virgin Queen.[99] Furthermore, she defended her position, e.g., through a divorce between her female body and her 'masculine' authority and power to be *King*.[100] The following reported speech[101] by Elizabeth I, of which there is some disagreement about the authentic words[102], nevertheless presents her *self-aggrandizement* strikingly:

> "I know I have the bodie, but of a weak and feeble woman, but I have the heart and Stomach of a King, [...] and think foul scorn that [...] any Prince of Europe should dare to invade the borders of my Realm [...] I my self will take up arms, I my self will be your General."[103]

Despite her own violation of the socially expected role of women, the Queen made sure that the social order in her kingdom stayed intact. The household was seen as the microcosm of the State and women's traditional subjection secured the civil order.[104]

Nevertheless, humanists claim for a classic education for aristocratic people also had an effect on aristocratic women. There was a steady increase of chances

---

[97] Cf. Valerius 152.

[98] Cf. Valerius 141.

[99] Cf. Valerius 240.

[100] Cf. Levin 121ff. ; cf. Rackin, *Tragic Audience* 275.

[102] Cf. Levin 206.

[103] Leonel Sharp. "Letter to George Villiers, Duke of Buckingham". N.d. [1623-5], *Cabala, Mysteries of State: In Letters of the Great Ministers of K. James and K. Charles,* 1654. 260. Rpt. in: "Topical Ideology: Witches, Amazons, and Shakespeare's Joan of Arc." Gabriele Bernhard Jackson. *Shakespeare and Gender: A History.* Ed. Deborah E. Barker, and Ivo Kamps. London: Verso, 1995. 153.

[104] Cf. Juliet Dusinberre, *Shakespeare and the Nature of Women.* London: Macmillan, 1975. 79.

for education for aristocratic women in Tudor England.[105] Tutors taught at home, and new found grammar schools could be visited.[106] Humanist's concern for a virtuous education of children additionally highlighted the responsibility of mothers to educate their children.[107] To fulfill this role, women had to be educated themselves.[108] From 1500 to 1600 evidence for an increase of education chances for aristocratic women could be found.[109] However, the development was not a steady increase but chances for education for women increased at first but declined during the last years.[110] Moreover, this development did not change the traditional separation between "the private (feminine) and public (masculine) spheres"[111].

3. Shakespeare's Theatre

Regarding Shakespeare's theatre, several differences in relation to modern theatres today can be pointed out. With respect to women, the main focus lies on the aspects which are essential to all theatres: the composition of the actors and their audience as well as their impact on the author and his plays.

3.1 The Actors

During Shakespeare's time, women were not allowed to be present on stage. *Boy-actors* were very popular who took women's and men's parts. Older characters, like e. g. Macbeth, were presumably played rather by men than boys. Nevertheless, all actors were male. In contrast to today's time, women's parts

---

[105] Cf. Valerius 153.

[106] Cf. Valerius 153.

[107] Cf. Dusinberre 206.

[108] Cf. Dusinberre 206.

[109] Cf. Valerius 168.

[110] Cf. Valerius 168.

[111] Rackin, *Shakespeare and Women* 9.

were expected and accepted to be played by *boy-actors*.[112] Furthermore, apart from scenes particularly designed to be humorous by the playwright, the *boy-actor's* performances were taken seriously and were seen as convincing.[113]

The reasons why only male actors were acknowledged raises the question why women were banned from the stage in the first place. Whereas other European countries during the same time accepted actresses on stage, like e. g. Spain, England strikingly adhered to the old tradition of male actors only.[114] Different assumptions were made to explain this traditional structure.

First, women were not meant to participate actively in Tudor England's public life.[115] A woman who provocatively rebelled against the strict rules of the social hierarchy in which men were supposed to be women's masters was considered to be *unnatural* in her behavior. To ban women from the stage is therefore the means to keep patriarchal structures intact and neglect any influence of women in public spheres. But a woman's temperament was not only seen as disturbing but could possibly lead to the accusation of being a witch.[116] As a matter of fact, women's *wrong* behavior seemed to be more threatening to Tudor and Stuart England's society than the, by writers often depicted, ugliness of women who were charged with witchcraft.[117] Also, Macfarlane had the impression that "[…] actions and personality, rather than physical factors, were the determining criteria"[118] for a woman to be accused of witchcraft. Moreover, Cañadas highlights:

---

[112] Cf. Rackin, *Shakespeare and Women* 74; cf. Callaghan 14.

[113] Cf. Rackin, *Shakespeare and Women* 74.

[114] Cf. Ivan Cañadas. *Public Theater in Golden Age Madrid and Tudor-Stuart London: Class, Gender and Festive Community.* Aldershot: Ashgate Publishing, 2005. 41ff.

[115] Cf. 2.2 *The Role of Women in the 16th and 17th Century.*

[116] Alan Macfarlane. *Witchcraft in Tudor and Stuart England. A Regional and Comparative Study.* London: Routledge, 1970. 161.

[117] Cf. Macfarlane 158.

[118] Macfarlane 158.

> "The negative emphasis authorities placed on female speech in prosecutions for witchcraft as well as common scolding contributed to the exclusion of women from the public stage in early modern England."[119]

For the contemporary organization of the social order was it therefore plainly inappropriate and against all female virtues if a real woman played not only an active role in a play but also presented herself in public.

Second, the general reputation of actors was low in the 16th and 17th century. For the reason that actors had to disguise themselves and did not show their real identities on stage, they were accused of lying. A document stating a contemporary opinion explained this assumption in the following way:

> "In Stage Plays for a boy to put on the attire, the gesture, the passions of a woman; for a mean person to take upon him the title of a Prince with counterfeit port, and train, is by outward signs to show themselves otherwise than they are, and so within the compass of a lie."[120]

According to this background, one of the reasons for keeping the professional acting companies' stages a male territory could have been that the actors wanted to gain more respect and improve their status[121]. Not only were men generally more valued in society but also male student acting groups, e. g., in Cambridge and Oxford, were seen as more professional than acting groups which toured the country and allowed women on stage.[122] However, this might have been one of the reasons for new professional companies to exclude women. Shakespeare's players eventually did not lack status. They gained the favor of Queen Elizabeth I quite quickly and were granted to play at court. Subsequently, James I. even bestowed the title "King's Men" on them when *The Lord Chamberlain's Men*, of

---

[119] Cañadas 44.

[120] E.K. Chambers. *The Elizabethan Stage* . Vol. 4. "Playes Confuted in Five Actions: 1582". Oxford: Clarendon, 1923. 217. Rpt. in: Rackin *Shakespeare and Women* 80.

[121] Cf. Rackin, *Shakespeare and Women* 42f.

[122] Cf. Rackin, *Shakespeare and Women* 43.

which Shakespeare was a member, enjoyed the King's patronage.[123] Despite the gained recognition, the former mentioned reason for keeping the professional companies male possibly played its part.

3.2 The Audience

Although women were not allowed on stage, they were present in Shakespeare's original audience.[124] Orgel points out that "foreigners visiting early modern London noted a considerable female presence at the public theaters"[125]. Furthermore, female spectators came from different social backgrounds, contemporary reports state that among them were "[…] applewives and fishwives, doxies and respectable citizens, queens and great ladies."[126] Even though women of different rank were documented spectators Shakespeare's theatres, the amount of documented records of women in the audience is scanty.[127] This fact is nevertheless not only true for women because neither male nor female spectators of low status were mentioned by name in Shakespeare's theatres but merely listed.[128] Paradoxically, Callaghan states that women of lower status visited the theatres more often than women of high rank.[129]

One would likely have guessed that famous female spectators like Queen Elizabeth, Queen Anne and different noble ladies must have been an attraction for

[123]Cf. Cook 7; cf. Vanessa Schormann. *Macbeth.* Hrsg. Sonja Fielitz. Bochum: Kamp, 2005. 37.

[124]Cf. Rackin, *Shakespeare and Women* 23; cf. Judith Cook. *Women in Shakespeare.* London: Harrap, 1980. 5.

[125] Stephen Orgel, *Impersonations: The Performance of Gender in Shakespeare's England.* Cambridge: Cambridge University Press, 1996. 10. Rpt. in: Cañadas 41.

[126] Andrew Gurr. *Playgoing in Shakespeare's London.* Cambridge: Cambridge University Press, 2004. Rpt. in: Rackin, *Shakespeare and Women* 25.

[127] Cf. Rackin, *Shakespeare and Women* 151; cf. Callaghan *Shakespeare Without Women* 160f.

[128] Cf. Callaghan 161.

[129] Cf. Callaghan, *Shakespeare Without Women* 161.

the Renaissance audience and that they presumably provoked a lot of attention.[130] Surprisingly, according to contemporary reports, women in general often gained the attention from male spectators who sometimes seemed to focus more on women in the audience than on the actor's performance.[131] Thus, women were not on stage but especially noticed by the audience anyway. This phenomenon seems to point again to the strict civil order in Tudor and Stuart England. For the reason that the female role in Shakespeare's time disputed women's participation in public life, women were usually excluded from public events or gatherings.[132] The attention that women in public provoked could therefore be for the rarity of their presence.

3.3 Shakespeare's Plays and the Contemporary Theatre

Looking at Shakespeare's plays, it is hardly recognizable that they were written, though for a mixed audience, for the performance of only male actors. Solely some indirect allusions indicate the original form of the plays' performance. E.g. , in *Antony and Cleopatra,* Cleopatra fears to be mocked by a *boy-actor* who represents her badly:

> "The quick comedians
> Extemporally will stage us and present
> Our Alexandrian revels; Antony
> Shall be brought drunken forth; and I shall see
> Some squeaking Cleopatra boy my greatness
> I'th' posture of a whore."[133]

Shakespeare's plays indicate at no point that they were exclusively written for male actors and neither do they exclusively focus on a male audience. Especially with regard to Shakespeare's tragedies, this statement can be verified according to contemporary documents. Rackin clarifies that

---

[130] Cf. Callaghan, *Shakespeare Without Women* 161.

[131] Cf. Cañadas 43.

[132] Cf. 2.2 *The Role of Women in the 16th and 17th century*.

[133] William Shakespeare, *Antony and Cleopatra.* Ed. John Wilders. *The Arden Shakespeare.* Gen. Ed. Richard Proudfoot, Ann Thompson and David Scott Kastan. London: Arden Shakespeare, 1995. 5.2.215-220.

> "[…] Renaissance audiences considered history plays depicting the valiant acts of […] forefathers to be aimed primarily at males, while tragedy, though aimed at both sexes, was determined 'to inspire womanly emotions in its spectators'."[134]

Reported emotional effects of tragedies on Shakespeare's audience like "compassion, remorse, pity"[135] etc. were labeled feminine as all emotions were categorized according to the social roles. However, tragedies were often described as

> "[…] appealing to women as well as men; and its appeal to men is repeatedly described as directed towards their feminine sympathies, softening hard hearts, piercing guilty souls with remorse, ravishing the entire audience with the feminine passions of pity and fear […]."[136]

Apart from tragedy's influences on the audience, evidence shows that Shakespeare's plays attracted male as well as female spectators during Renaissance times as well as they do today. The art of choosing telling characters, fascinating themes and highly effective scenes for a performance on contemporary stages which are as effective on modern stages as they were then, marks Shakespeare's excellence.

4. Analysis of Selected Women Characters in *Romeo and Juliet*, *Macbeth* and *Antony and Cleopatra*

4.1 *Romeo and Juliet*

4.1.1 Plot Summary

The play takes place in Verona and Mantua at the beginning of the 15th century. The families "Montague" and "Capulet" live in Verona and are feuding since many years. However, Romeo, the son of the Montague clan, falls deeply in love with Juliet, the young daughter of the Capulet family. Juliet falls in love with Romeo as well. Despite the hatred that exists between their families, the young lovers choose to follow their hearts. They secretly get married by Friar Laurence,

---

[134] Rackin, *Engendering the Tragic Audience* 266.

[135] Cf. *Introduction* 1.

[136] Rackin, *Engendering the Tragic Audience* 266.

who hopes that through their marriage the long-lasting enmity between the families can be resolved. But fate plays its part. Tybalt, Juliet's cousin, meets Romeo and his friend Mercutio on a street in Verona and insults the young Montague. Mercutio draws his sword. Romeo keeps his countenance but as Tybalt stabs Mercutio, he kills Tybalt in revenge for killing his friend. Romeo has to flee from Verona to Mantua for this reason, but he nevertheless spends the wedding night with Juliet. Juliet is confronted with her parent's plan for her to marry Paris, a kinsman of the Prince of Verona. When the Nurse, Juliet's accomplice in her secret wedding, advises Juliet to forget Romeo, Juliet uses her last option and talks to Friar Laurence. He figures out a plan to save Juliet from her unwanted marriage with Paris and to reunite her with Romeo. Juliet must drink a potion that puts her into a death-like sleep for forty-two hours. After drinking it, she should be entombed and will awake after a certain period of time. Romeo would be informed by a letter from Friar Laurence's plan so that the young lovers can flee from their family's feud when Juliet awakes. On the day when she is supposed to marry Paris, she drinks the potion and appears to be dead. She gets entombed in the cemetery of her family according to the Friar's plan. However, Romeo does not receive the letter from Friar Laurence. When Romeo hears about Juliet's death, he buys a vial of poison from an Apothecary and hurries to her tomb in order to die next to his love. At the Capulet crypt he sees Paris and kills him in a swordfight. Then, he dies by Juliet's side. When Juliet awakes, she sees her lover Romeo lying dead next to her. After a kiss on his poisonous lips does not kill her, she reaches for his dagger and commits suicide. Called by the churchyard watchman, the Prince of Verona, the Capulet clan and Montague, Romeo's father, arrive at the tomb where Friar Lawrence tells the lovers' tragic story. Devastated by their children's death, the heads of the Capulet and Montague families decide to resolve the long blood feud and declare peace between them.

4.1.2   Analysis of Important Female Characters

4.1.2.1 Juliet

Juliet is a thirteen year old girl who, at the beginning of the play, does not think about marriage or love yet.[137] When her mother suggests her to consider the marriage with Paris, a kinsman of the Prince of Verona, she obediently assures her mother to do so during an arranged ball.

> "I'll look to like, if looking liking move,
> But no more deep will I endart mine eye
> Than your consent gives strength to make it fly." (*Rom.* 1.3.97 – 99)

As the age implies, she not only behaves but also thinks like a girl rather than like a woman. Her conception of marriage and love seems to be naïve and obviously not thought-through. When she meets Romeo, her development to a stronger, more individual character begins. Whereas she was dominated by her parents and the Nurse and her advice of evaluating future husbands, she now develops her own ideals. Juliet does not want to conform to expected norms anymore as soon as her love for Romeo comes alive. She realizes her own personal interpretation of love and marriage which lets her appear more mature and marks the change for her to become a woman and more importantly an independent personality. The development of her character, from a naïve girl to a self-confident woman, can also be seen in the language she chooses. The pronounced insecurities in her behavior in the first balcony scene can be regarded as indicators for her very young age.[138]

> "O gentle Romeo,
> If thou dost love, pronounce it faithfully.
> Or, if thou think'st I am too quickly won,
> I'll frown and be perverse and say thee nay,

---

[137] Cf. William Shakespeare. *Romeo and Juliet*. Ed. Brian Gibbons. *The Arden Shakespeare*. Gen. Ed. Richard Proudfoot, Ann Thompson and Scott Kastan. London: Arden Shakespeare, 1980. 1.3.13-15; 1.3.64-66.

[138] Cf. Leech, Clifford. "The Moral Tragedy of 'Romeo and Juliet.'" *English Renaissance Drama: Essays in Honor of Madeline Doran & Mark Eccles*. Ed. Standish Henning, Robert Kimbrough, and Richard Knowles. Southern Illinois University Press, 1976. 59-75. *Shakespeare for Students: Critical Interpretations of "As You Like It", "Hamlet", "Julius Caesar", "Macbeth", "The Merchant of Venice", "A Midsummer Night's Dream", "Othello", and "Romeo and Juliet"*. Ed. Mark W. Scott. Detroit: Gale, 1992. 508.

So thou wilt woo; but else, not for the world.
In truth, fair Montague, I am too fond,
And therefore thou mayst think my haviour light,
But trust me, gentleman, I'll prove more true
Than those that have more cunning to be strange." (*Rom.* 2.2.93-101)

Moreover, Juliet's youth is displayed by her allegory of a child's treatment of a *wanton's bird* compared to hers towards Romeo and by her comic revelation of calling him for no reason.

"'Tis almost morning, I would have thee gone,
And yet no farther than a wanton's bird,
That lets it hop a little from his hand
Like a poor prisoner in his twisted gyves,
And with a silken thread plucks it back again,
So loving-jealous of his liberty." (*Rom.* 2.2.176 -181)

Juliet:	"I have forgot why I did call thee back.
Romeo:	Let me stand here till thou remember it.
Juliet:	I shall forget, to have thee still stand there,
	Remembering how I love thy company."(*Rom.* 2.2.170-173)

Furthermore, she explains that she calls Romeo in a low voice because she does not want to risk being caught by her father. In this context, she mentions her father's guardianship over her by saying "Bondage is hoarse and may not speak aloud, […]" (*Rom.* 2.2.160). This comment obviously manifests her dependence on her father, her social status as his daughter and therefore her position of a child.

Next to the *wanton's bird,* she uses another image of child-like behavior and compares it with her own while she is waiting for Romeo to arrive on their wedding night.

"So tedious is this day
As is the night before some festival
To an impatient child that hath new robes
And may not wear them."(*Rom.* 3.2.28-31)

However, this comparison seems more distant from herself than the first one and merely seems to display Juliet's memory for she is maturing as she speaks.[139] In

---

[139] Cf. Leech 509.

the course of Act 3 Juliet's believes are her own and not influenced by the Nurse or her family anymore. Several scenes prove Juliet's growing independence. E. g., Juliet refuses to believe the Nurse's report and her interpretation of the news that Juliet's cousin Tybalt was killed by Romeo. After the Nurse ends her accusing speech with "Shame come to Romeo" (*Rom.* 3.2.89), Juliet protests it:

> "Blister'd be thy tongue
> For such a wish. He was not born to shame.
> Upon his brow shame is asham'd to sit,
> For 'tis a throne where honour may be crown'd
> Sole monarch of the universal earth.
> O, what a beast was I to chide at him."(*Rom.* 3.2.90-95)

She is sure of her love for Romeo and trusts him. She tries to avoid the marriage with Paris although it is scheduled by her parents and supported by the Nurse. She is not convinced to agree to marry Paris by the Nurse's reports about the County's looks and is not held back by the feud that exists between Romeo's and her family. For her, the ideal of true love, disregarding all obstacles, becomes the goal to strive for. For this reason, she plans on fleeing with Romeo from the dominating views of her parents and the Nurse. She trusts Romeo fully and chooses the dangerous and courageous way of imitating her death in order to free her from the unwanted marriage and a life without her true love.

4.1.2.2 The Nurse

> "Let any man conjure up in his mind all the qualities and peculiarities that can possibly belong to a nurse, and he will find them in Shakespeare's picture of the old woman [...]."[140]

Besides this quotation of how early criticism regarded the Nurse's nature, she is an important female character in the tragedy next to Juliet. The Nurse became Juliet's wed nurse, when her own baby died eleven years ago. She stayed close to the Capulet family and took care of Juliet while she was growing up. The Nurse's husband died, so Juliet seems to mean everything to the Nurse. She seems to have a closer relationship to Juliet than her mother has. On the one hand, this is implied

---

[140]Cf. Samuel Taylor Coleridge. "Extracts from a report by J. P. Collier of a lecture given by Coleridge (1811-1812)". *Shakespeare's Early Tragedies: "Richard III", "Titus Andronicus" and "Romeo and Juliet"; A Casebook.* Ed. Neil Taylor and Bryan Loughrey. London: Macmillan, 1990. 36.

by Juliet confiding her secret love affair with Romeo to her. On the other hand, the language in which Juliet talks to her mother in Act 1 is rather formal and implies a certain distance, e. g., by addressing her as "Madam" (*Rom.* 1.3.6).[141]

The Nurse also has a comical purpose in the play. Her remarks and speeches are often inappropriate and therefore lead to humorous scenes. She also teases Juliet oftentimes with bawdy remarks, e.g., after she arranged Romeo and Juliet's marriage:

Nurse: "I am the drudge and toil in your delight
But you shall bear the burden soon at night." (*Rom.* 2.5.75-76)

Apart from that, in Juliet's secret affair and later on marriage, the Nurse at first is her loyal companion. She furthermore states that it is her wish to see Juliet married once. (Cf. *Rom.* 1.3.61-62) Moreover, the Nurse has an important role as the messenger between the young lovers as it is also stated by Stevens[142]. Only through her help can Romeo and Juliet's romance stay a secret at the beginning and only through her support can the secret marriage take place. In Act 3, Scene 5, her major influence on arranging the marriage with Romeo is described. She instructs Juliet

Nurse: "Then hie you hence to Friar Lawrence's cell.
There stays a husband to make you a wife."(*Rom.* 2.5.69-70)

In Act 3, Scene 4, the Nurse protects the young lovers furthermore from getting caught when they are secretly talking through an open window of Juliet's chamber to which Romeo climbed up. Thus, it is the Nurse who informs Juliet that her mother is on her way to her chamber and that the young lovers have to beware that they will not get caught. (Cf. *Rom.* 3.5.39-40)

---

[141] Cf. Dash 70.

[142] Cf. Martin Stevens. "Juliet's Nurse: Love's Herald." *Papers on Language & Literature*, 2.3 (1966): 195-206. Rpt. in *Shakespeare for Students: Critical Interpretations of "As You Like It", "Hamlet", „Julius Caesar", "Macbeth", "The Merchant of Venice", "A Midsummer Night's Dream", "Othello", and "Romeo and Juliet"*. Ed. Mark W. Scott. Detroit: Gale, 1992. 514ff.

Nevertheless, the Nurse totally disagrees with Juliet's view of love and marriage. In contrast to Juliet, she believes in a more earthly and factual love. Furthermore she does not appear to be a deep-thinking woman. The Nurse's main interest of the secret wedding seems to be her own wish: to see her now "only child" Juliet happily married. But when the obstacles against Juliet's and Romeo's love become too huge and a marriage between Paris and Juliet is already planned by her parents, the Nurse gives Juliet the advice to forget Romeo and marry Paris instead.

> "Romeo is banish'd, and all the world to nothing
> That he dares ne'er come back to challenge you.
> Or if he do, it needs must be by stealth.
> Then, since the case so stands as now it doth,
> I think it best you married with the County." (Cf. *Rom.* 3.5.213-217)

It seems that the "good, sweet Nurse" (*Rom.* 2.5.21), as Juliet calls her in the beginning, has only Juliet's best interest in mind by giving her this advice. The Nurse's view of marriage is of a more material and practical sort than Julia's[143]. From her perspective, a wealthy man who is moreover handsome must be a "man of wax" (*Rom.* 1.3.76), meaning, he must be a faultless husband. Under the aspects of security and a peaceful life that would be given to Juliet by marrying Paris and taking the parent's hatred against the Montague family into account, the Nurse's advice is best for Juliet according to her earthly and realistic thinking.

> "O, he's a lovely gentleman.
> Romeo's a dishclout to him. An eagle, madam,
> Hath not so green, so quick, so fair an eye
> As Paris hath. Beshrew my very heart,
> I think you are happy in this second match,
> For it excels your first; or, if it did not,
> Your first is dead, or 'twere as good he were
> As living here and you no use of him."(*Rom.* 3.5.218-225)

It is therefore incomprehensible for her to understand Juliet's ideal of passionate love because her understanding of love is of the opposite nature. It is a natural consequence that Juliet rejects her old confidante for advising her to break her

---

[143] Cf. Stevens 516.

marriage vows and prefer Paris over her husband. After the Nurse has left the stage she decides: "Thou and my bosom henceforth shall be twain" (*Rom.* 3.5.240). Juliet furthermore shows her disappointment by calling her a "most wicked fiend!" (*Rom.* 3.5.236).

As well as the contradicting views of love and marriage, also the Nurse's obscene language contrasts Juliet's style of expressing herself.[144] Therefore, Juliet and the Nurse are often seen as comic "foils"[145] to another.[146]

4.1.3. The Role of Women Represented in *Romeo and Juliet*

At the beginning of the play, Juliet's character corresponds to the expected social role of a daughter in an aristocratic family in Elizabethan England. She is expected to be obedient to her parents and to agree to their wishes. She therefore speaks to her mother in a formal way and even agrees to the thought of marrying a husband chosen by her parents. Her specifically young age plays an important role in the play and is furthermore linked to an Italian tradition. For the reason that the tragedy plays in Verona, Italy, also Italian customs are included. It seems to be tradition that aristocratic daughters, like Juliet, married at the age of thirteen or even earlier in 15th century Italy. Or at least in the play it is Lady Capulet's argument for her daughter to consider marriage:

> *Lady Capulet*: "Younger than you
> Here in Verona, ladies of esteem,
> Are made already mothers. By my count
> I was your mother much upon these years
> That you are now a maid." (*Rom.* 1.3.69-73)

In contrast to this, scholars believe that in late Elizabethan England, the average age for daughters to marry was generally older, and assumingly around the age of

---

[144] Cf. Scott 461.

[145] "A foil is a character who through strong contrast underscores or enhances the distinctive traits of another character." Scott 461.

[146] Cf. Scott 461.

twenty.[147] Furthermore, childbirth was considered as dangerous for girls as young as Juliet is in the play.[148] Dash observes that

> "Although the setting is Verona, the relationship of a teenage daughter with her elders – her mother, father, and Nurse – has a universality not limited to a particular place".[149]

And strikingly, some similarities with the Elizabethan civic order can nevertheless be found. In the course of the play, the presentation of Juliet, with regard to her obedience to her parents, changes. By falling in love with Romeo and secretly marrying him, she disregards her mother's advice of marrying Paris. Her alliance with the hostile Montague family disrespects her parent's authority and could easily be seen as a traitorous act by her family. She not only secretly acts according to her own feelings when it comes to the love of Romeo but also eventually disagrees with her parent's opinion and especially with the head of the Capulet household. This presumably seemed as an *unnatural* act to the Elizabethan audience, as even the wife was supposed to respect and obey her husband's wants. The fight between Juliet and her parents, especially with her father, can be regarded as more dramatic for a Renaissance audience than for a modern one. Although a child's good behavior is valued in our society, the need for independent choices of a child is a respected norm. However, Juliet pronounces her opinion to her mother and does not obey to her parent's wish to marry Paris:

Juliet: "I pray you tell my lord and father, madam,
I will not marry yet. And when I do, I swear
It shall be Romeo, whom you know I hate,
Rather than Paris." (*Rom.* 3.5.120-123)

Nevertheless, she cannot win over her father's dominance. The rules and roles are obvious: Juliet is under the guardianship of her father and she cannot make her own decision because they are made for her by the head of the household. The

---

[147] Cf. Dash 68-69.

[148] Cf. Dash 68-69.

[149] Dash 71.

unnaturalness of Juliet's disobedience is displayed by her father's threat of casting her out of her paternal home.

Capulet:	"Hang thee young baggage, disobedient wretch!
	I tell thee what – get thee to church a Thursday
	Or never after look me in the face.
	Speak not, reply not, do not answer me.
	My fingers itch. Wife, we scarce thought us blest
	That God had lent us but this only child;
	But now I see this one is one too much,
	And that we have a curse in having her.
	Out on her, hilding." (*Rom.* 3.5.160-168)

Capulet:	"To answer 'I'll not wed, I cannot love,
	I am too young, I pray you pardon me!'
	But, and you will not wed, I'll pardon you!
	Graze where you will, you shall not house with me.
	Look to't, think on't, I do not use to jest.
	Thursday is near. Lay hand on heart. Advise.
	And you be mine I'll give you to my friend;
	And you be not, hang! Beg! Starve! Die in the streets!
	For by my soul I'll ne'er acknowledge thee,
	Nor what is mine shall never do thee good.
	Trust to't, bethink you. I'll not be forsworn." (*Rom.* 3.5.185-195)

In contrast to Juliet, the Nurse thinks the marriage with Paris will be her better and furthermore only option after this fight with Capulet. The Nurse is not only a "perfect depiction of a nurse"[150] but she also represents the common belief of marriage in Shakespearean times. For a woman to marry out of love was in Elizabethan England a very rare circumstance. Marriage was merely a business arrangement to gain status and wealth through, which was especially important in aristocratic families. As Juliet is from an aristocratic family as well, her 'fate' of marriage is already determined by her parents. Moreover, Juliet is the only heiress of her respected family and the future husband who will gain her wealth should be therefore carefully chosen by her father.[151]

---

[150] Cf. Coleridge 36.

[151] M. M. Mahood, *Wordplay in Romeo and Juliet.* (London: 1957). 56-72. Ed. Taylor, Neil and Loughrey, Bryan, eds. *Shakespeare's Early Tragedies: "Richard III", "Titus Andronicus" and "Romeo and Juliet"; A Casebook.* London: Macmillan, 1990. 36.

Capulet: "Earth hath swallow'd all my hopes but she;
She is the hopeful lady of my earth." (*Rom.* 1.2.14-15)

When Lady Capulet asks Juliet to consider the marriage with Paris, who she will see on the following ball, it is already a hint from her mother to get used to the thought of the probably upcoming marriage with the County. It is not, how Juliet might have interpreted it, in her power to decide if she marries Paris or not; it is solely an information from her mother to get acquainted with her future husband. Although the Nurse supports Juliet in keeping her affair and her marriage with Romeo secret, she does not dare to generally contradict the opinion of Capulet, the head of the family. The Nurse nevertheless tries to protect Juliet from her father's anger over Juliet's disobedience:

Nurse: "God in heaven bless her!
You are to blame, my lord, to rate her so." (*Rom.* 3.5.168-169)

The Nurse is quickly put in her place when Capulet says:

Capulet: "Peace you mumbling fool!
Utter your gravity o'er gossip's bowl,
For here we need it not." (*Rom.* 3.5.173-175)

The audience becomes aware of the fact that the Nurse is only the family's servant and for this reason of very low status. For a servant to profoundly disagree with the master is a very courageous action of which the Nurse is not capable of. This demonstration of the family hierarchy might have also influenced the Nurse's decision to advise Juliet of the lesser of two evils according to her interpretation of the situation. Like Lady Capulet, the Nurse accepts the restricted role of women in the family by remaining obedient. Her materialistic and earthly thinking furthermore stops her from supporting Juliet's dream-like ideal of true love. From the background of the Nurse's Elizabethan perception of marriage, and the father's threat to let Juliet "starve on the streets" if she does not obey, the Nurse gives Juliet the advice that she thinks is best for her under the circumstances:

Nurse: "Beshrew my very heart,
I think you are happy in this second match,
For it excels your first; or, if it did not,
Your first is dead, or 'twere as good he were
As living here and you no use of him."

Juliet: "Speakest thou from thy heart?"

Nurse: "And from my soul too, else beshrew them both." (*Rom.* 3.5.221-227)

By rejecting her parent's and Nurse's advice, Juliet can now be seen as an independent woman who follows her own wishes and under no circumstances wants to commit bigamy, a disgraceful crime and the cause of God's damnation as seen by the Elizabethan audience. Furthermore, she is determined to follow her heart disregarding social norms and expectations. The passionate Juliet is willing to die for her goal of loyal love which eventually seems inevitable to her.

4.2 *Macbeth*

4.2.1   Plot Summary

The play takes place in Scotland and in England around the middle of the 11th century.[152] Macbeth and Banquo, two successful generals of Duncan, the king of Scotland, meet three witches on a heath while returning from a victorious battle. The witches prophesy them their future. Therefore, Banquo should be the father of many kings whereas Macbeth shall become thane[153] of Cawdor and eventually king of Scotland. The witches vanish, and Macbeth and Banquo treat their prophecies suspiciously when a messenger arrives and pronounces that Macbeth is named thane of Cawdor by King Duncan. After this incident, Macbeth considers the witches' third prophecy and writes a letter to his wife telling her about the witches' prophecy and his ambitious wish of becoming king. King Duncan is expected to be a guest in Macbeth's castle that night. Lady Macbeth encourages her husband to fulfill his wish and convinces him to kill the sleeping king while he is a guest in Macbeth's castle. Her plan is that the king's two chamberlains should be made drunk by her so they won't notice what will happen during the night. Macbeth should kill the sleeping king and the next day, the chamberlains should be made responsible for the deed. Macbeth follows her wife's instructions and kills the sleeping King Duncan, using the daggers of the king's chamberlains.

---

[152] "The historical Macbeth reigned in Scotland from 1039 to 1056 A.D." Cook 120.

[153] "In *Scottish Hist.* A person, ranking with the son of an earl, holding lands of the king; the chief of a clan, who became one of the king's barons". *The Oxford English Dictionary.* 2nd ed. Vol. 17. Oxford: Clarendon, 1989. 863.

Lady Macbeth also smears the sleeping servant's faces with Duncan's blood in order to be able to suspect them in the morning. Macduff, a nobleman of the king, discovers the deed the next day. When the chamberlains get suspected, Macbeth kills them allegedly out of rage. Malcolm and Donalbain, the former king's sons, flee to England and Ireland because they fear for their own lives as heirs of the throne. Macbeth is crowned the new king and blames Malcolm and Donalbain for the regicide. Banquo, who knows about the witches' prophecy and who should be the father of a line of kings, is an immediate threat to Macbeth's crown. Therefore, Macbeth hires a group of murderers to kill him and his son Fleance. When Fleance escapes the murderous attack, Macbeth is in constant fear for his crown. His fears haunt him so much that he even envisions the ghost of the dead Banquo sitting on his chair during a feast. He reacts to his hallucination, startling his guests and almost giving away his crime through it. As a last resort, Macbeth visits the witches again. They warn him of Macduff but also promise him that nobody born of woman could harm him and that he was safe until Birnam Wood came towards Dunsinane Castle. Macbeth is falsely relieved believing that a forest cannot move and every man is born of woman. When Macduff flees to England, Macbeth regards him as a traitor and orders to kill his family that he left behind. When Macduff hears about the murder of his wife and children, he seeks revenge. In the meantime, Lady Macbeth cannot bear the guilt of the regicide, becomes insane and starts walking in her sleep. In a sleepwalking scene, she gives her cruel crime away. While being unconscious, she tries to wash the imagined blood of the deed from her hands. Also Macbeth cannot flee from his guilt. Malcolm and Macduff raise an English army and lead it towards the Dunsinane Castle. The soldiers hide themselves with branches from the Birnam Wood so that it seems like the wood moves towards the castle. Macbeth is still willing to fight. When the death of his wife is announced to him, he does not have many words for her. The English army arrives at the castle and when Macduff explains, while dueling Macbeth, that he was born by Caesarean section, Macbeth loses his courage for a moment but keeps fighting until Macduff kills him. Malcolm eventually becomes the new righteous king.

4.2.2   Analysis of Important Female Characters

4.2.2.1 Lady Macbeth

Lady Macbeth is one of Shakespeare's most power seeking, ambitious, scary but also one of the most famous female characters. When Macbeth trusts her with his immoral ambition to become forcefully king, she shares his ambition of gaining power. She decides without further hesitation or moral scruples to support her husband with the fulfillment of his immoral wish.

Lady Macbeth: "Hie thee hither,
That I may pour my spirits in thine ear,
And chastise with the valor of my tongue
All that impedes thee from the golden round,
Which fate and metaphysical aid doth seem
To have thee crown'd withal."[154]

She is excited and only sees the promised golden future that Macbeth indirectly promises her in his letter.

Lady Macbeth: "Thy letters have transported me beyond
This ignorant present, and I feel now
The future in the instant." (*Mac.* 1.5.56-58)

By saying this, Lady Macbeth forgets that in order to be in her desired future "There is another very unpleasant instant preceding it which has to be acted on – the murder of Duncan."[155] But she is so thrilled by their royal future that she is determined to do anything for it, disregarding the means. Without further ado, she starts to plan the quickest way to their promised future. At this point, it is questionable if Lady Macbeth only desires her husband to become king and wants to see him glorious, or if she is furthermore also considering and longing for her own powerful status of being queen of Scotland. Lady Macbeth never mentions

---

[154] William Shakespeare. *Macbeth.* Ed. Kenneth Muir. *The Arden Shakespeare.* Gen. Ed. Richard Proudfoot, Ann Thompson and David Scott Kastan. London: Routledge, 1984. 1.5.25-30.

[155] Stephen Spender. "Books and the War – II." *Shakespeare for Students: Critical Interpretations of "As You Like It", "Hamlet", "Julius Caesar", "Macbeth", "The Merchant of Venice", "A Midsummer Night's Dream", "Othello", and "Romeo and Juliet".* Ed. Mark W. Scott. Detroit: Gale, 1992. 261.

her own ambition for power and status, but emphasizes her husband's glorious career. (Cf. *Mac.* 1.5.54-55) For the reason that she never leaves her role as Macbeth's wife and never seeks power individually but only for him, Lady Macbeth can be regarded as motivated by her love for her husband with the respect that she wants to see him crowned king.

In order to commit the murder, which is necessary to gain the crown, Lady Macbeth is aware that her womanly virtues would only stop her from fulfilling her and her husband's wish. At this point Lady Macbeth, unlike her husband, does not think critically about the plotted murder. Without a doubt, she calls upon the evil forces in her ambitious speech to take her good womanly virtues from her and *unsex her*. She wishes to become *manly* determined so she could commit the regicide herself:

> "Come, you Spirits
> That tend on mortal thoughts, unsex me here,
> And fill me, from the crown to the toe, top-full
> Of direst cruelty! make thick my blood,
> Stop up th'access and passage to remorse;
> That no compunctious visitings of Nature
> Shake my fell purpose, nor keep peace between
> Th'effect and it! Come to my woman's breast,
> And take my milk for gall, you murth'ring ministers,
> Wherever in your sightless substances
> You wait on Nature's mischief! Come, thick Night,
> And pall thee in the dunnest smoke of Hell,
> That my keen knife see not the wound it makes,
> Nor Heaven peep through the blanket of the dark,
> To cry, 'Hold, hold!' " (*Mac.* 1.5.40-54)

In her speech, the evil spirits should help her to free herself from all her good *female* virtues and replace them with pure cruelty. In a way, she allies with the witches.[156] Her demand that the spirits should *unsex* her reminds the audience of the witches, because also they are neither male nor female:

Banquo: "you should be women,
And yet your beards forbid me to interpret
That you are so."(*Mac.* 1.3.45-47)

---

[156] Cf. Janet Adelman. "'Born of Woman': Fantasies of Maternal Power in 'Macbeth.'" *Shakespeare for Students: Critical Interpretations of "As You Like It", "Hamlet", "Julius Caesar", "Macbeth", "The Merchant of Venice", "A Midsummer Night's Dream", "Othello", and "Romeo and Juliet"*. Ed. Mark W. Scott. Detroit: Gale, 1992. 285-286.

When Macbeth tells his wife that he does not want to perform the regicide, Lady Macbeth urges him to do it by questioning his love for her and furthermore his braveness, his credibility and his manhood. She represents in this part the controlling *male* role in the relationship.

Lady Macbeth:	"From this time Such I account thy love. Art thou afeard To be the same in thine own act and valour, As thou art in desire? Would'st thou have that Which thou esteem'st the ornament of life, And live a coward in thine own esteem, Letting 'I dare not' wait upon 'I would,' Like the poor cat i'th'adage?"
Macbeth:	Pr'ythee, peace. I dare do all that may become a man; Who dares do more, is none.
Lady Macbeth:	"What beast was't then, That made you break this enterprose to me? When you durst do it, then you were a man; And, to be more than what you were, you would Be so much more the man." (*Mac.* 1.7.38-51)

Lady Macbeth knows her husband so well that her argumentation shows its effects. Macbeth also applies the same argument when he wants to persuade and hire a group of men to kill Banquo. In that scene, Macbeth questions their manhood by comparing the men with dogs and challenging them by saying only men prove to be men in "violently self-assertive action"[157].

Lady Macbeth plots King Duncan's murder and pushes her husband further into fulfilling their ambitious wishes. She earlier expects that her husband is "[…] too full o'th'milk of human kindness, To catch the nearest way" (*Mac.* 1.5.17-18) and kill the good king. She therefore uses a cruel imagery that contrasts her to Macbeth, implying that she was even more masculine in her behavior than he is:

"I have given suck, and know
How tender 'tis to love the babe that milks me:
I would, while it was smiling in my face,
Have pluck'd my nipple from his boneless gums,
And dash'd the brains out, had I sworn
As you have done to this." (*Mac.* 1.7.54-59)

---

[157] Ramsey, Jarold. "The Perversion of Manliness in 'Macbeth.'" *Shakespeare for Students: Critical Interpretations of "As You Like It", "Hamlet", "Julius Caesar", "Macbeth", "The Merchant of Venice", "A Midsummer Night's Dream", "Othello", and "Romeo and Juliet"*. Ed. Mark W. Scott. Detroit: Gale, 1992. 263-266.

This speech also implies that her former demand to get filled with male cruelty shows its effects. Although she does not act out what she says, her mind is full of cruel images and lacks human kindness. Eventually, after her call upon the evil forces and the cruel imagery, she manipulates Macbeth successfully to commit the regicide. When he is on his way, she confesses to the audience that she had been too weak to do it herself, because King Duncan would resemble her father when he sleeps. (Cf. *Mac.* 2.2.12-13) This is one example of the dominating theme in her character: It seems like the two conflicting forces of her womanly virtues and devilish ambitions are both present in her character. Whether ambition dominated at the beginning of the play, e. g. during the persuasion of her husband, her suppressed female qualities and her *human kindness* become more powerful and arouse an overwhelming remorse for her murderous ambition in the end. This contradiction implies Macbeth when he says that she is a masculine soul inhabiting a female body. Ambition and violence seems to be linked to masculinity in the play.

At the beginning, Lady Macbeth definitely appears to be the stronger part in the crime. When Macbeth returns from murdering the king, she tries to calm her husband's bad conscience. When Macbeth notices that he still holds the murder weapons in his hands, he is too shocked from his own deed that he is too afraid to go back to the scene of the crime. Therefore, it is Lady Macbeth who hides the evidence. Lady Macbeth smears the chamberlain's faces with Duncan's blood which covers their daggers, so that they can be suspected of killing the king in the morning.

But, like her character, also Lady Macbeth's relationship to her husband changes during the play. At the beginning, they are presented as a trusting couple, sharing each other's thoughts. In his letter, Macbeth addresses Lady Macbeth even as "my dearest partner in greatness" (*Mac.* 1.5.11). But as the play proceeds and the killings do not seem to stop, Lady Macbeth and her husband become more and more estranged from each other. It seems like each character suffers from the huge guilt alone and in different ways. Macbeth tries to secure his reign by killing all his enemies who he is afraid of. In contrast to that, Lady Macbeth longs for the killings to stop and is furthermore not informed about her husband's plans and actions anymore. She starts to walk in her sleep. During her sleepwalking soliloquy she shows her deep concerns:

> "The Thane of Fife had a wife: where is she
> now? – What, will these hands ne'er be clean? –
> No more o'that, my Lord, no more o'that: you mar
> all with this starting." (*Mac.* 5.1.40-43)

She does not know about her husband's arranged murders anymore and can only assume them from their outcome. (Cf. *Mac.* 3.2.45-46) Lady Macbeth does not necessarily suffer more of the regicide's guilt than Macbeth but definitely in a different way because she becomes helpless and insane. During her sleep and her sleepwalking she cannot control her guilty conscience anymore. She only sleeps with candlelight for she is afraid of the dark but even this does not help her troubled mind. Over and over again she relives the same scene in her sleep: herself trying to wash her hands clean from a bloodstain left from the regicide. Immediately after the deed was performed, she does not seem aware of her enormous guilt and seems to feel innocent despite the murderous crime.

> "My hands are of your colour; but I shame
> To wear a heart so white." (*Mac.* 2.2.63-64)

Ironically, the image that she could so easily pronounce in Act 2, Scene 2, and that she used to soothe her husband's mind, does now haunt her:

> "A little water clears us of this deed:
> How easy is it then!" (*Mac.* 2.2.66-67)

Lady Macbeth's guilty conscious kills her in the end. She cannot cope with the guilt of the regicide and is overwhelmed by the thought that her husband keeps killing to secure his reign. She cannot soothe her conscience anymore and commits suicide out of despair. Although her husband wishes that she had "died hereafter" (*Mac.* 5.5.17), he does not lament her death in particular, for his life on the whole seems worthless to him: "Life's but a walking shadow; […] / […] it is a tale / Told by an idiot, full of sound and fury, / Signifying nothing" (Mac. 5.5.24; 26-28).

Eventually, the audience is reminded of the devious heroine by Malcolm's final soliloquy, calling her a "fiend-like Queen, Who, as 'tis thought, by self and violent hands Took off her life" (*Mac.* 5.9.35-37).

4.2.2.2 Lady Macduff

Lady Macduff contrasts Lady Macbeth's role in its complete construction. She is an obedient woman, not seeking for power and lacking independence. When Macduff leaves his family behind, Lady Macduff thinks that her husband does not love his family because of his departure:

Lady Macduff:	"[…] to leave his wife, to leave his babes, His mansion, and his titles, in a place From whence himself does fly? He loves us not." (*Mac.* 4.2.6-8)

Lady Macduff is warned by a messenger that Macbeth ordered a group of murderers to slaughter Macduff's family. She nevertheless stays at the house and blames her husband for not protecting them:

"The most diminutive of birds, will fight,
Her young ones in her nest, against the owl." (*Mac.* 4.2.10-11)

She is helpless and fearful without her husband and completely dependent on him. She stays at home, ironically almost waiting for the murderers to arrive.

Lady Macduff:	"Whither should I fly? I have done no harm. But I remember now I am in this earthly world, where, to do harm Is often laudable; to do good, sometime Accounted dangerous folly: why then, alas! Do I put up that womanly defence, To say, I have done no harm?" (*Mac.* 4.2.72-78)

Even if Lady Macduff realizes her *womanly defence* will not help her, she is caught in her female role as the good Elizabethan housewife.

Although Lady Macduff only once occurs in the play and does not have significant influence on the plot, she is a striking contrast to Lady Macbeth, who embodies the mighty evil female role. In contrast to Lady Macbeth, Lady Macduff represents the good and weak female role. The good as embodied by Lady Macduff and her children is weak in the play's society and shows the unnatural order under the reign of a tyrant. In contrast to Lady Macbeth, Macduff's wife and her children are helpless and any violent behavior is completely absent. Whereas Lady Macbeth comes close to the border to manliness in her speeches, e. g., by demanding the evil spirits to *unsex her* and *take her milk for gall*, Lady Macduff stays put in her traditional female role and gets slaughtered innocently without further resistance.

The one scene in Lady Macduff's house provides the only domestic sphere apart from Macbeth and Lady Macbeth's home. Whereas Lady Macduff's house is a place of the good, Macbeth's house is the contrary: a haunted house of evil.

4.2.3   The Role of Women Represented in *Macbeth*

Lady Macbeth completely turns the socially expected norms of Elizabethan accepted beliefs about women around. She appears to an Elizabethan audience as the female incarnation of the devil – driving her husband to commit regicide, a highly immoral and unnatural deed. Furthermore, the king is a guest in Macbeth's castle that night. Macbeth realizes himself:

Macbeth: "He's here in double trust:
First, as I am his kinsman and his subject,
Strong both against the deed; then, as his host,
Who should against his murderer shut the door,
Not bear the knife myself." (*Mac.* 1.7.12-16)

The double trust refers to the fact that King Duncan is a guest in Macbeth's castle and Macbeth is his subject, which, he realizes, are strong reasons against the murder. Macbeth's confidante, Lady Macbeth, anyway persuades him of committing the cowardly deed of stabbing the king while he's sleeping. Her behavior contradicts here enormously the believed role of the woman as the "giver of life and nourishment"[158].

Her call for the evil spirits, her demand to become less womanly and more evil in her soliloquy and her wish for a dark night to commit the murder all lets the Elizabethan audience associate her with witchcraft.[159] Witchcraft as well as the possession of daemons were supernatural forces that the audiences in Shakespeare's England believed in.[160] Lady Macbeth's unnatural perversion of her femininity with respect to her actions, links her close to the described bisexuality of the witches. Macbeth also realizes her *male* character traits when he pronounces "thy undaunted mettle should compose / Nothing but males" (*Mac.* 1.7.73-75).[161] In hindsight Lady Macbeth's greeting of Macbeth: "Great Glamis! Worthy Cawdor! / Greater than both, by the all-hail hereafter" (*Mac.* 1.5.54-55), reminds the audience sound-wise of the greeting of the witches, whereas Macbeth does not seem to notice it.[162]

Although Lady Macbeth demands to become filled from head to toe with cruelty, she cannot deny her female nature. The evil forces seem to fight with her female virtues at times. The sleeping Duncan who she cannot kill because he reminds her of her father marks one *female* aspect in her behavior. And most of all, her concerns and her despair in the sleepwalking scene describe her womanly emotions that come to the surface when she cannot control them, during her sleep. The witches' prophecy again seems to become true: "Fair is foul, and foul is fair" (*Mac.* 1.2.11) - all former civil order seems to be turned upside down and nothing seems to be like it was. Lady Macbeth advises her husband to "look like the innocent flower, / But be the serpent under't" (*Mac.* 1.5.65-66). She performs this

---

[158] Irving Ribner. "'Macbeth': The Pattern of Idea and Action." *Shakespeare for Students: Critical Interpretations of "As You Like It", "Hamlet", "Julius Caesar", "Macbeth", "The Merchant of Venice", "A Midsummer Night's Dream", "Othello", and "Romeo and Juliet".* Ed. Mark W. Scott. Detroit: Gale, 1992. 245.

[159] Cf. Märtin 148.

[160] Cf. Märtin 148.

[161] Cf. Märtin 148-149.

[162] Cf. Märtin 150.

strategy perfectly herself from the beginning, e. g., when King Duncan compliments her at a time when she is already determined to kill him. (Cf. *Mac.* 1.6.23-24) Moreover, the natural order of things is flouted in general which is displayed by several unnatural events in nature. (Cf. *Mac.* 2.4. 6-7; 10-20) By the end of the play, Macbeth even disregards the social role of women as accepted in Shakespeare's time by making women fight in his army. (Cf. *Mac.* 4.3.186-188) The natural order which was believed in during Shakespeare's time gets completely perverted. This has a disturbing effect on all areas that are displayed in the play.

The loving relationship between Macbeth and Lady Macbeth at the beginning is unusual for Elizabethan times. When Macbeth informs Lady Macbeth, his "dearest partner in greatness", about his secret thoughts and addresses her kindly with "My dearest love" (*Mac.* 1.5.58), "dearest chuck" (*Mac.* 3.2.45) etc., a trusting love relationship between the characters is displayed. Only through their closeness can Lady Macbeth have so much power over Macbeth. Without his wife, Macbeth's moral had stopped him from committing the regicide. Again, this relationship of the main characters is seen *unnatural* for Shakespeare's audience. The hierarchical order of husband and wife with different social roles was expected. Arranged marriages based on respect rather than love were the norm. When Shakespeare knew about the Humanistic ideal which, despite the maintaining of different roles in society, proclaimed the equality of partners in marriage, *Macbeth* had definitely been a critique of this ideal. Only through the close relationship between the protagonists can Lady Macbeth gain so much power over her husband. She questions his love for her and he proves himself *manly* ambitious for her through the regicide. Although Lady Macbeth is only presented in the domestic sphere, which was appropriate for women in contemporary England, her affinity to supernatural forces marks her *unnatural*. Regarding this finding, Lady Macbeth can be seen as a warning symbol for Shakespeare's audience. Not only is she emotionally close to her husband so she can control and manipulate his actions, which can be marked as a critique of the Humanistic ideal of marriage; but she also symbolizes a woman possessed by daemons or witchcraft and her devilish actions as well as her eventual tremendous suffering of her decision to call the evil spirits works as a warning against all *unnatural* behavior of women.

Doctor of Physic:	"[…] Unnatural deeds Do breed unnatural troubles: infected minds To their deaf pillows will discharge their secrets. More needs she the devine than the physician." (*Mac.* 5.1.68-71)

Lady Macbeth's fall and her early decision to evil and immorality reflects the Elizabethan belief in the woman in general. The common belief was that the role of women is to be obedient to the man in all areas, because she is more easily tempted by the immorality which refers back to the Fall of Man in Genesis I. Lady Macbeth seems to be a reminder for the Elizabethan audience of this social hierarchy that needs to be intact in order to prevent chaos and unnatural occurrences in the State. Despite Lady Macbeth's strong influence on Macbeth and on the course of the play, her power is seen as evil. With regard to Lady Macbeth, the play displays an indirect warning of women for they are too easily tempted by immoral actions. Therefore, a woman in Elizabethan England should not be granted too much power.

Lady Macduff specifically represents the role of the accepted obedient role of women. She is helpless without her husband and is unable to defend herself alone. All violent behavior is foreign to her and she is unable to make her own decisions. When Lady Macduff is warned that murderers are on the way to her house, she is still unable to take action. She neither flees with her children, nor does she prepare to defend herself. Although she realizes that her *womanly defense* of pretending her innocence will not help her in a world where evil rules, it seems that she cannot act independently from her husband. Lady Macduff is included in the reverse order of the witches' prophecy which is acted out by Macbeth: "Fair is foul, and foul is fair" (*Mac.* 1.2.11). Although, Lady Macduff is acting according to her social role, she gets innocently slaughtered by the evil tyrant. In a world where the natural order is perverted, good old values cannot survive.

Conclusively, especially the role of Lady Macbeth in *Macbeth* is a very complex character which gives room for several different interpretations. The most important criticism with regard to women however can be found in the display of the horrible supernatural influences on human beings as well as the necessity of the hierarchical and natural structure of woman to man in order to prevent chaos in domestic as well as in public areas. The display of devilish possession or witchcraft seems to have been a great fascination in Shakespeare's time in which supernatural powers like witchcraft and the possession of daemons were believed in.[163] The effect of supernatural powers displayed must have been a sensation. Nevertheless, the play seems timeless. In modern audiences, the characterization and self-reflective thinking of the protagonists including the depiction of a criminal's remorse seems to capture the audience's interest in modern audiences even more.

4.3 *Antony and Cleopatra*

4.3.1   Plot Summary

The play takes place in the year 40 B. C. when, after Julius Caesar's death, Mark Antony, Octavius Caesar and Lepidus rule the Roman empire. When the play opens, Mark Antony spends some time in Egypt where he conducts an affair with the experienced Egyptian Queen Cleopatra. The information of the death of his wife, Fulvia, reminds him of his former duties in Rome. He manages to escape Cleopatra's charm and returns to Rome to reconcile with his co-rulers in order to regain political power. For this reason, he even marries Octavius Caesar's sister Octavia to secure his bond with Caesar. Reunited, the triumvirs meet Pompey and settle their differences without going to battle. However, Caesar does not keep the peace and imprisons Lepidus for treason and fights Pompey victoriously on his own. Mark Antony is angered by this occurrence. Furthermore he is drawn to Cleopatra again. When a confrontation between Antony and Caesar seems unavoidable, Octavia leaves Antony and returns to her brother in Rome. Antony returns to Egypt and starts to raise a huge army to fight Caesar. Caesar, who is furious

---

[163] Cf. Märtin 148.

about Mark Antony's betrayal, sends troops to Egypt in order to fight Antony's and Cleopatra's army. During the battle at sea, Cleopatra's ship flees cowardly and Mark Antony's follows her lead, leaving the rest of the fleet susceptible. At a second battle, again the Egyptian fleet abandons the fight so that Caesar's fleet defeats Antony's. Mark Antony, believing in Cleopatra's treachery, is determined to kill her. But when he is informed about Cleopatra's suicide, which she counterfeited, he is struck by grief and admiring her honorable act he attempts to join her in death. When he hears that Cleopatra is still alive, he urges his guards to be brought to her while suffering from a deadly wound. He eventually dies next to her. After the defeat, Cleopatra refuses to be shown in Rome as a victory sign for Octavius Caesar and chooses the only way to escape this fortune: She requests several poisonous snakes which put her to death while she presents herself as the queen of Egypt: crowned and in her royal attire.

4.3.2 Analysis of Important Female Characters

4.3.2.1 Cleopatra

Cleopatra is one of Shakespeare's most complex characters and it seems that she is "constant only in constantly changing"[164]. Differing interpretations about her character are therefore possible.

The most contradicting poles in her character seem to be on the one hand her role of the influential Egyptian queen and on the other hand the female lover in the relationship with Antony. In love as in politics, Cleopatra uses her emotional decisiveness, her playfulness and her charm to get her way. Despite her womanly nature, her power over rulers and lovers seems exceptional.

Whether she seduces the powerful Antony or is angry at her apparently disloyal servant: Her actions are effective presentations of her emotional nature. Enobarbus, one of Antony's followers, describes her influence by saying "Age

---

[164] Dash 85.

cannot wither her, nor custom stale / Her infinite variety" (Ant. 2.2.245-246). Antony realizes her *infinite variety* as well and depicts her calling her a

> "[…] wrangling queen,
> Whom everything becomes – to chide, to laugh,
> To weep; whose every passion fully strives
> To make itself, in thee, fair and admired!" (*Ant.* 1.2.49-52)

Her enemies in Rome are threatened by her power and her games she likes to play. Having seduced and allied with Julius Caesar before, she is not only a threat to the Roman's kingdoms but furthermore to their pride and honor. Cleopatra is not only a strong woman but also a powerful ruler. From the Roman perspective, Cleopatra's character is therefore regarded as very negative. According to the Roman generals, the Egyptian queen robs Antony of his reputation and lets him forget his duties and makes him "the noble ruin of her magic" (*Ant.* 3.10.19). Enobarbus hardly ever sees Cleopatra in her political role as the queen of Egypt but mostly as an emotional and seductive woman. He imagines Cleopatra's reaction to Antony's departure from Rome to be the following:

> "[…] Cleopatra, catching but the
> least noise of this, dies instantly. I have seen her die
> twenty times upon far poorer moment." (*Ant.* 1.2.147-149)

After Fulvia's death, he tells Antony not to lament about his loss because his new love Cleopatra would be more attractive.

> "[…] your old smock brings
> forth a new petticoat, and indeed the tears live in an
> onion that should water this sorrow." (*Ant.* 1.2.175-177)

Enobarbus not only describes Cleopatra as emotional but he also comments on the reasons for her emotional outbursts. Although he tells Antony that he assumes that her reaction to his departure would be genuine, he also mentions that if this was not the case, it would be just as impressive and effective.

> "[…] her passions are made of
> nothing but the finest part of pure love. We cannot
> call her winds and waters sighs and tears; they are
> greater storms and tempests than almanacs can report.
> This cannot be cunning by her. If it be, she makes a
> shower of rain as well as Jove." (*Ant.* 1.2.153-158)

The Romans describe her as an immoral "gipsy" (*Ant.* 1.1.10) at the very beginning of the play and later on as "Egyptian dish" (*Ant.* 2.6.128). Caesar even labels her a "whore" (*Ant.* 3.6.68). As a queen, she is seen as in no sense harmless. Pompey speaks of her and her behavior as "Salt Cleopatra [...] / Let witchcraft join with beauty, lust with both" (*Ant.* 2.1.21-22).

Against the Roman portrayal of her, Cleopatra's is much more than a seductive woman. As a queen she advises Antony to "Hear the ambassadors" (*Ant.* 1.1.49) in the first scene. But Antony focuses only on his love for her and sends the diplomats away, explaining his decision by saying it was "for the love of Love, and her soft hours" (*Ant.* 1.1.45).

Her shows are always impressive, e. g., she is once described of not just walking through the street but performing her presence.

Enobarbus: "I saw her once
Hop forty paces through the public street
And, having lost her breath, she spoke and panted,
That she did make defect perfection,
And, breathless, pour breath forth." (*Ant.* 2.2.238-242)

But her games and her true or forged self-presentations are not only effective in their performance but also in their expected responses to it. When Antony's departure is dawning on her, she says

"See where he is, who's with him, what he does.
I did not send you. If you find him sad,
Say I am dancing; if in mirth, report
That I am sudden sick. Quick, and return." (*Ant.* 1.3.3-6)

Cleopatra is well aware of the fact that she shows herself enigmatic with her unpredictable behavior and unforeseeable actions. When Charmian, one of her female attendants, advises her to be obedient and gain Antony's heart through it, she resolutely repudiates her suggestion.

Charmian: "Madam, methinks if you did love him dearly,
You do not hold the method to enforce
The like from him.

Cleopatra:	"What should I do I do not?"
Charmian:	"In each thing give him way; cross him in nothing."
Cleopatra:	"Thou teachest like a fool: the way to lose him." (*Ant.* 1.3.7-10)

Although Cleopatra is Antony's mistress, she is not ashamed to discuss the matter. As Egypt's ruler she must have learned not simply to trust the man's decision but to use her knowledge against him in order to get her way. She pressures him by saying:

Cleopatra:	"What, says the married woman you may go? Would she had never given you leave to come!" (*Ant.* 1.3.21-22)
Cleopatra:	"Oh, never was there queen So mightily betrayed! Yet at the first I saw the treasons planted." (*Ant.* 1.3.25-27)
Cleopatra:	"Why should I think you can be mine and true – […] Who have been false to Fulvia? Riotous madness, To be entangled with those mouth-made vows Which break themselves in swearing!" (*Ant.* 1.3. 28; 30-32)

Cleopatra uses the marriage vows here as means of exerting pressure, although her own understanding that the bond of marriage is irreversible could be implied here as well. In everything she does she is breath-taking. She perfectly knows the game of deception.

According to Cleopatra's will, Antony does pronounce his love for her in saying "I go from hence / Thy soldier, servant, making peace or war / As thou affects" (*Ant.* 1.3.70-72). This early in the play, Antony's dependence on Cleopatra is displayed by these words. With regard to his position, it is appropriate to make this speech as her lover but inappropriate concerning his status as part of the triumvirs and his sudden status as widower. Cleopatra points this out. When Antony does not lament his wife's death openly, she provokes him by advising him a deceiving behavior which had suited her own strategy of trickery.

"I prithee, turn aside and weep for her,
Then bid adieu to me, and say the tears
Belong to Egypt. Good now, play one scene
Of excellent dissembling, and let it look
Like perfect honour." (*Ant.* 1.3.76-81)

Cleopatra still feels betrayed by Antony's departure. She makes clear with the former provocation that Antony should not confuse his tears of Fulvia's death with his tears of leaving her. "O most false love!" (*Ant.* 1.3.63) she judges. As well as Antony shows his bond to Cleopatra, the Egyptian queen shows her two-sided character. She switches into her queen mode when she disregards her former emotional "folly" and says goodbye to Antony.

Cleopatra: "Your honour calls you hence;
            Therefore be deaf to my unpitied folly,
            And all the gods go with you!" (*Ant.* 1.3.99-101)

While Antony returns to the Roman world of male domination, Cleopatra longs for her lover (Cf. *Ant.* 1.5). Blatantly, she makes sexual remarks about her past lover Julius Caesar (Cf. *Ant.* 1.5.30-35) and Antony: "O, Charmian, / Where think'st thou he is now? […] / […] is he on his horse? / O happy horse, to bear the weight of Antony!" (Ant.1.5. 19-20; 21-22). In contrast to her emotional longing, Antony rationally allies with Caesar again and even marries his sister Octavia for the reason to keep the alliance intact. Antony, who claims to be Cleopatra's "servant", suddenly loses his loyalty to her in Rome where Caesar degrades her by calling her "a slave" (Cf. *Ant.* 1.4.19).

Cleopatra is sure of Antony's love for her. She compares him to a fish that is caught by her (Cf. *Ant.* 2.5.11-14*)*. But when Cleopatra hears about Antony's marriage she shows her jealousy by even striking her innocent messenger down and threatening him further. Eventually, she realizes her own part in angering Caesar:

Cleopatra: "In praising Antony, I have dispraised Caesar."
Charmian: "Many times, madam."
Cleopatra: "I am paid for't now." (*Ant.* 2.5. 108-109)

Cleopatra shows her wit as a political woman in these lines. She knows Octavius Caesar, and assumes correctly that he had an impact on the arranged marriage between Antony and Octavia for it secures Antony's political bond with Caesar and divides him from Egypt. Antony nevertheless decides to go back to Cleopatra: "And though I make this marriage for my peace, / I'th' East my pleasure lies" (*Ant.* 2.4.38-39). Cleopatra is convinced that Antony will come back to her after a messenger describes Octavia to her and she assumes her to be "Dull of tongue and dwarfish" (*Ant.* 3.3.16).

Continuously, Cleopatra shows her political awareness. Through the affair with Antony she gains "lower Syria, Cyprus and Lydia" (Ant. 3.6.10). Against Enobarbus pleading, Cleopatra also goes to battle with Antony. She supports his decision to which Caesar challenges him: to fight by sea. Antony calls her Thetis[165] for that reason. Although a Soldier and Canidius, one of Antony's followers, plead him to fight at land he sticks to his decision. Canidius concludes: "So our leader's led, / And we are women's men" (*Ant.* 3.8.69-70), implying that Cleopatra and her woman are about to lead the battle. When Cleopatra's ship flees from battle, she explains her behavior as an action led by fear. Cleopatra shows herself here as a fearful woman rather than a ruler. When Antony blames her for leading him from the battlefield and to defeat, Cleopatra excuses herself over and over again:

Cleopatra:	"O, my lord, my lord, Forgive my fearful sails! I little thought You would have followed." (*Ant.* 3.11.54-56)
Cleopatra:	"Oh, my pardon!" (*Ant.* 3.11.61)
Cleopatra:	"Pardon, pardon!" (*Ant.* 3.11.68)

The Roman perception of her increases in its negativity and even Antony seems to be determined of her betraying nature. When Caesar sends a messenger to Cleopatra she charmingly speaks with him but does not conform to Caesar's will of sending Antony out of her country. Antony chides her for being charming

---

[165] *Thetis* is "a see-goddess and the mother of Achilles. The term is appropriate for Cleopatra because of her support for the expedition by sea and her association with a great warrior". *The Arden Shakespeare: Antony and Cleopatra.* 197.

and for granting her hand kissed by the messenger. He lets him get whipped. Before the second battle at sea, Cleopatra helps Antony to put on his armor which Griffin fittingly describes as "a stage picture suggesting the paintings of Venus arming Mars."[166]

In the second battle at sea Cleopatra's fleet flees again which leads to Antony's second defeat. However, if the fleet's behavior was determined by Cleopatra or by the situation in the battle is questionable. Antony believes in Cleopatra's betrayal. He is enraged, calls her a "gipsy" (*Ant*. 4.12.28) and a "Triple-turned[167] whore!" (*Ant*. 4.12.13), and although he depends on Cleopatra's goodwill, he swears:

> "The witch shall die.
> To the young Roman boy she hath sold me, and I fall
> Under this plot. She dies for't." (Ant. 4.12.47-49)

Cleopatra is afraid, barricades herself and sends Antony the misleading report of her suicide. Hearing this, Antony wants to do her alike in order to regain his honor and be reunited with Cleopatra, who he seeks to ask for forgiveness. He then falls on his sword but does not die immediately. When one of Cleopatra's attendants informs him that Cleopatra is still alive, he demands to be brought to her in order to show his love for her

> "I am dying, Egypt, dying. Only
> I here importune death awhile until
> Of many thousand kisses the poor last
> I lay upon thy lips." (*Ant*. 4.15.19-22)

Even in this emotional scene, Cleopatra shows her dominance over Antony. When he further asks to speak, it is Cleopatra who announces: "No, let me speak" (*Ant*. 4.15.45). But Cleopatra shows herself as formative as loving. After Antony died, she speaks about her love for him and her grief firstly in her role as a woman, secondly as Egypt's queen:

---

[166] Alice Griffin. *Shakespeare's Women in Love*. Raleigh: Pentland, 2001. 142.

[167] *Triple-turned* in the sense of "From Julius Caesar to Gnaius [sic!] Pompey, from Pompey to Antony, and, as he now suspects, from him to Octavius Caesar" *The Arden Shakespeare: Antony and Cleopatra*. 250.

> "No more but e'en a woman, and commanded
> By such poor passion as the maid that milks
> And does the meanest chares. It were for me
> To throw my scepter at the jujurious gods
> To tell them that this world would did equal theirs
> Till they had stolen our jewel." (*Ant.* 4.15.77-82)

Even later on, she daydreams of Antony, imagining him to be a glorious emperor and showing her love for him through it.

Cleopatra: "I dreamt there was an emperor Antony.
                     O, such another sleep, that I might see
                     But such another man! […]
                     His face was as the heavens, and therein stuck
                     A sun and moon which kept their course and lighted
                     The little O, the earth. […]" (*Ant.* 5.2.75-77; 78-80)

Nevertheless, she secures her own triumph over Octavius Caesar's plan in the end. In order to prevent to be remembered and presented in Rome as the defeated "whore" (Cf. *Ant.* 5.2.220) of Egypt, she shows herself being "marble-constant" (*Ant.* 5.2.239) and determined in her goal: demanding "Give me my robe. Put on my crown. I have / Immortal longings in me" (*Ant.* 5.2.279-280). By presenting herself as Egypt's queen, she finally secures her immortal dignity through her death. Before she dies, she moreover shows his love for Antony by calling "Husband, I come!" (*Ant.* 5.2.286)

4.3.2.2 Octavia

Octavius Caesar's sister Octavia becomes Mark Antony's second wife. Octavia is obedient to her brother, conforming to his wish of marrying Antony. Octavia is humble and forgiving. When Antony informs her that he will be absent from her for political reasons, she simply assures him that she will pray for him then (Cf. *Ant.* 2.3. 1-4). Octavia is a minor female character which shows a contrast to the female protagonist Cleopatra. Octavia never criticizes Antony and although he implicitly promises her to be loyal:

> "My Octavia,
> Read not my blemishes in the world's report.
> I have not kept my square, but that to come
> Shall all be done by th' rule" (*Ant.* 2.3.4-7),

he nevertheless leaves her for the Egyptian queen. Enobarbus describes Octavia as "of a holy, cold and still conversation." (*Ant.* 2.6.124-125) and Menas asks "Who would not have his wife so?" (*Ant.* 2.6.126). It is obvious here that Octavia corresponds to the concept displayed of an ideal Roman wife: She is humble and obedient and of a still conversation. She does not seem to have a temper like Cleopatra, she also is not as provocative but neither is she as strong and decisive nor as seductive as Cleopatra. Antony's *pleasure* lies in Egypt whereas his duties lie in the Roman world of which one part is being Octavia's husband. It seems that also Octavia sees the marriage as a duty that she has to fulfill. She *weeps* when she has to leave Octavius Caesar for her husband (Cf. *Ant.* 3.2.42). When she hears about the upcoming enmity between Antony and Caesar, she shows her despair:

Octavia:	"Praying for both parts. The good gods will mock me presently When I shall pray 'O, bless my lord and husband!'; Undo that prayer by crying out as loud 'O, bless my brother!' Husband win, win brother, Prays and destroys the prayer; [...]" (*Ant.* 3.4.14-19)

Torn between her loyalty to Antony and to Octavius Caesar, she chooses her brother over her husband and returns to Caesar.

4.3.3   The Role of Women Represented in *Antony and Cleopatra*

Cleopatra contradicts the whole perception of women in Elizabethan England. She is powerful, independent and very critical. She is a sensual lover to Antony and a calculated ruler of Egypt. She deceives Egypt's enemies and stays miraculous until the end. Her role includes power, perceived as *male* in Shakespeare's England, and emotional love, which was seen as the essence of femininity. Cleopatra combines these poles in a round character. She is self-conscious and uses her *womanly* character traits like fearfulness and emotional outbursts for her advantage.

The audience in Shakespeare's time had probably associated Cleopatra's role with the role that Queen Elizabeth I played in their everyday life. Also she was a female ruler in times when the social order was patriarchal. Cleopatra's role contrasts the Roman world which is dominated by men and male virtues. Whereas Queen Elizabeth gave up her life as a woman for a life as England's queen and appeared as the "Virgin Queen", married to her country, Cleopatra includes both parts in her character. Shakespeare shows which effects this decision has on her reputation. The Egyptian queen is surrounded by women and under her servants merely a Eunuch can be found, no man. Egypt is presented as governed by a woman and furthermore influenced and dominated by female virtues. The Roman world displays the opposite: three male rulers share their governance. And the Romans mock the female sovereign. In the Roman patriarchal society women were seen to be inferior to men. This view corresponds with the Elizabethan society's understanding. Therefore, the Romans do not criticize Cleopatra as the Egyptian monarch but simply in her role as a woman. Here, the impossibility is presented that a female ruler in a patriarchal society, as in Shakespeare's times, can only remain her sovereignty by denying her dependence on men and by becoming a god-like ruler or comparable to a saint, e. g., like Elizabeth I presented herself as the "Virgin Queen" reminding society of the "Virgin Mary". The climax of this dualism is shown in Cleopatra's death. In Elizabethan England, the woman was seen as weaker and, because the woman was the cause for the Fall of Men, a woman was seen as more easily tempted by immorality. Only in her death, Cleopatra regains her immortal royal honor and dignity. Through her denial of her role as woman she proves her royal strength as a monarch:

> "My resolution's placed, and I have nothing
> Of woman in me. Now from head to foot
> I am marble-constant. Now the fleeting moon
> No planet is of mine." (Ant. 5.2.237-240)

Apart from the dualism of her different roles, Cleopatra is often accused by critics as the only reason for Antony's fall. Although Cleopatra had an impact on keeping Antony away from Rome, the essence of his fall lies, however, in the different cultural worlds that they represent: the *feminine* Egypt versus the *masculine* Rome. Kahn appropriately points out:

"In his passion for Cleopatra, he "o'erflows the measure," escapes the mold, and crosses the boundary between Roman and Other. By thus violating the cultural codes in which masculinity is written, he risks the loss of his very identity."[168]

With regard to the relationship between Antony and Cleopatra their equality of status is moreover striking. Even Antony describes himself and Cleopatra in the beginning as "a mutual pair" (Ant. 1.1.38). Despite the fact that their relationship is immoral and *unnatural* for the Elizabethan audience because it is not legalized by marriage, it is furthermore highly immoral and religiously unacceptable in terms of infidelity. In their relationship male and female behavior is displayed by both partners and the role of the other sex causes insecurities displayed by each character. Cleopatra goes to war which is *unnatural* and disturbing for the Elizabethan audience that believed war to be men's business. Cleopatra flees from the battlefield womanly, out of fear, as she states, and Antony confesses to her "See / How I convey my shame out of thine eyes / By looking back what I have left behind / 'Stroyed in dishonour" (3.11.51-54) after following her. He feels "robbed of his sword" (Cf. *Ant.* 4.14.23) when her navy leaves him to defeat a second time. The changing of their social roles is symbolized in Cleopatra's seemingly harmless game:

> "I drunk him to his bed,
> Then put my tires and mantles on him, whilst
> I wore his sword Philippan." (*Ant.* 2.5.21-23)

Antony's manhood is questioned and he is torn between his "pleasure" in Egypt which undermines his male honor and dignity and his role as a successful emperor in Rome. After Antony followed Cleopatra's ship, one of his followers judges over his action:

> "I never saw an action of such shame.
> Experience, manhood, honour, ne'er before
> Did violate so itself." (*Ant.* 3.10.22-24)

Also Cleopatra's honor and dignity is at stake for she has an affair with a man who is married, even if to different women in the course of the play. As soon as Antony is in Egypt though, he provokes Caesar to fight him in order to regain his

---

[168] Kahn 116.

manly honor. Kahn suitably points out "Shakespeare's Roman heroes strive to prove themselves men not in relation to women, but against a rival [...] by competing against [him] with the aim of excelling and dominating."[169]

His actions therefore lead to the final doom of Antony and his lover. Nevertheless, Cleopatra plays the stronger role in the relationship. Whereas Antony at the beginning can manage to leave her domination, he is again dependent on her when he returns to Egypt. A woman as a dominant part in a relationship that is immoral and damnable according to the religious belief in Shakespeare's England was revolutionary material in Renaissance England.

The role of Octavia corresponds to Elizabethan norms of the behavior of women. Her marriage is arranged by her brother Caesar and he marries her off to Antony who he formerly chides. The simple reason for this marriage is the alliance between Antony and Caesar which Octavia dutifully accepts. Octavia is obedient and follows her brother's or her husband's wish as she is supposed to according to the Elizabethan patriarchal structure. Even when Antony did her wrong, she neither confronts him nor does she stand in his way. She simply leaves and returns to Caesar who takes politically revenge on Antony for dishonoring his sister. As well as the marriage merely functions as a security of the political alliance with Antony for Caesar, so does he react in a political sense with war against his cousin. Caesar simply asks Octavia to be patient: "Pray you / Be ever known to patience" (*Ant.* 3.6.99-100). This manifests the passiveness that she is forced to and which is her expected virtue. Even though Octavia is the sister of the mighty Octavius Caesar, as a powerless and role-conforming woman she stays permanently at her brother's mercy.

The greatest criticism that the play displays is against a marriage without love. Both of Antony's marriages, the one with Fulvia as well as with Octavia were simple arrangements. Like in the Elizabethan world, to marry for reasons of love was very rare. In the play, Fulvia and Antony's brother fight Caesar and Antony denies engaging in the war. As a result, Fulvia dies. Because also in his second marriage Antony does not act loyal to his wife, a new war breaks out, this time

---

[169] Kahn 15.

against him. "Why did he marry Fulvia and not love her? / I'll seem the fool I am not. Antony / will be himself" (*Ant.* 1.1. 42-44). In these lines, Cleopatra clearly displays her view of marriage. Through Antony's disloyal behavior he loses his reputation in Rome and furthermore provokes his downfall.[170]

5. Comparative Analysis of Juliet, Lady Macbeth and Cleopatra

5.1 Similarities

Regarding the three women characters Juliet, Lady Macbeth and Cleopatra, some similarities and a lot of differences can be ascertained. Beginning with the similarities, all of them are not only self-confident but also loving and tragic female characters who rebel against society's norms.

All three characters are presented as self confident women: Juliet, speaking against her father's opinion and following her own ideal of marriage, Lady Macbeth, determinedly leading Macbeth to fulfill his ambitious desires against his scruples and Cleopatra, the essence of self-conscience, criticizing her lover Antony for his infidelity and staying sure of his love for her despite his marriage with Octavia. Obviously, the three female protagonists are to be seen with respect to their lovers, as their self-confidence can be measured towards their behavior to their partners.

The theme of love is present in all three tragedies although the women characters display it in different ways. The love between Juliet and Romeo is of an innocent nature. Romeo, once feeling like "fortune's fool" (*Rom.* 3.1.138), depicts here a theme that is always present in their relationship: fate. Juliet is overwhelmed by her feelings that she acts according to her prediction that if Romeo swears to love her she would "no longer be a Capulet" (Rom. 2.2.35-36). Through her attempt to escape their social constraints by surfeiting her death, she shows her

---

[170] Cf. Griffin 141.

determination. It is a young love that Shakespeare puts on stage. Even though it contradicts their family's plans for them, their love can be regarded as pure and innocent. Neither wealth nor possessions, not even security does this love offer. Juliet and Romeo fight for the mere realization of their love against all adversities.

The love that exists between Lady Macbeth and her husband is of a different sort. As a thane's wife, Lady Macbeth lives in certain prosperity. When Macbeth fights in the battlefield, she waits for him in their castle and is informed about the events through his letters to her which she responds. Their love seems secure and throughout the play they stay loyal to each other. Shakespeare does not give away if Lady Macbeth ever had children but in this marriage the couple is childless. Lady Macbeth shares her husband's ambition for power and influence. Mysteriously paralleled with the language and the bad influence of the witches, Lady Macbeth's "love" for her husband drives him to regicide. Therefore, this love cannot be labeled as innocent in comparison to Juliet's love for Romeo. They become partners in crime and through Lady Macbeth's influence, her husband puts ambition over morality, which soon provokes the end of their love.

Cleopatra's love is contrasting and resembling parts of each love concept at the same time. On the one hand, she is sure of Antony's love for her and even when he marries Octavia in Rome she believes in his return to Egypt. On the other hand, Cleopatra is deceiving. In contrast to Lady Macbeth, she does not always value Antony's actions and ambitions. Whereas Lady Macbeth denies her identity in order to help her husband achieve his ambitious and highly immoral goal, Cleopatra literally leaves her lover to his own defeat. Cleopatra shows her affection for Antony. Nevertheless, her political self contradicts this love for him. After his death, she acknowledges her adoration and praises him gloriously as a successfully emperor. It seems, although she does love Antony despite his betrayal, she never forgets her responsibilities for her country and her own independence.

Moreover, all three women characters contrast accepted norms in the play which strikingly resemble the rules of the patriarchal social order in Elizabethan England. Juliet rebels against the domination of her father, Lady Macbeth flouts all morality by driving her husband to murder and Cleopatra rules her country without denying her womanly self. Eventually, the women characters have a tragic ending in common: they commit suicide, each of them motivated by different reasons.

Taking these similarities into account, it is obvious that although these similar features are present, they are revealed in different situations and in different contexts. Respecting the differences that these three female protagonists show a broadening development of character from Juliet to Lady Macbeth to Cleopatra can be discovered.

5.2 Character Development

Juliet, Lady Macbeth and Cleopatra are three characters who represent women in different stages in their lives. Their development can be detected in their public, private and political or calculative behavior.

Juliet is the youngest character. Being thirteen years old, she is under her father's guardianship and not supposed to make decisions on her own. Her influence is therefore highly restricted. She can marry her first love Romeo only secretly and with the help of the Nurse. Her status, although being from an aristocratic family, is relatively low as a daughter. When she speaks against her father's opinion, her low status which dictates her to obey becomes obvious. She eventually cannot change her father's decision to marry her to a husband that he chose for her. Her father even threatens her to throw her out of the parental home if she does not obey. Juliet has to choose between either being bound to a man who she does not love and betraying her secret husband Romeo, or being neglected by her own family and to be homeless. Juliet is as a daughter who is totally dependent on her father's will and therefore powerless.

Lady Macbeth is a woman of middle age, who, at the opening of the play, is married to Macbeth, the *Thane of Glamis*. When her husband is fighting in battle, she stays in their castle is granted a certain degree of independence while he is gone. Through her status as the wife of a thane she has the control over her servants and is respected in society. Lady Macbeth is not only older than Juliet but furthermore settled and more influential.

Cleopatra shows the highest level of public influence. She is the Queen of Egypt and the mother of Julius Caesar's son, Caesarean. She is the oldest of the three female protagonists. As a monarch, her status and power is majestic. She rules Egypt as its sovereign and even leads it to war against the Roman Empire. Her public influence is overwhelming.

Also in the domestic and private area the same pattern occurs. Juliet is presented as the least experienced woman. Her first and only lover is Romeo who she secretly marries.

In contrast to Juliet, Lady Macbeth was married before and Macbeth is her second husband. Although she mentions a baby in her rhetoric (Cf. *Mac.* 1.7.54-55), the information is contradicted by Macduff later on in the play (Cf. *Mac.* 4.3.216). Lady Macbeth most likely is childless. The marriage between her and Macbeth is definitely "barren" which the missing heir for King Macbeth proves (Cf. *Mac.* 3.1.60-61). Lady Macbeth is moreover bound to her domestic role. She is experienced in being a housewife and takes charge in the domestic sphere. Lady Macbeth's shows her enormous private influence on her husband's actions by driving him to regicide. This is where her most influential power lies, in the privacy of their relationship.

Cleopatra exceeds the other female characters in her experience. Although she preserves her independence and is displayed in the tragedy as unmarried, she engages in affairs with influential rulers like Julius Caesar and Mark Antony. Moreover, she is the mother of Caesarean, Julius Caesar's son. Throughout the play, Cleopatra is depicted as beautiful and deceiving. She seems to be admired and feared at the same time because of her charming but deceptive nature.

In their political power and calculative behavior respectively, the developing structure of the characters stays coherent.

Juliet makes a pact, firstly with the Nurse and secondly with Friar Laurence, in order to secretly marry Romeo and attempt to escape the unwanted marriage with Paris. For the reason that the sole effect of these pacts is the maintenance of Juliet's secret love affair, the arrangements cannot be regarded as calculative political thinking. It shows simply Juliet's ability to keep her secret love alive with the help of her accomplices: the Nurse and the Friar.

Contrasting Juliet, Lady Macbeth makes a more influential pact with the witches by calling them to help her to "unsex her" (*Mac.* 1.5.41) and fill her with "direst cruelty" (*Mac.* 1.5.43) in order to drive her husband to the regicide. Despite her secret alliance, she pretends her innocence after the deed in public. When the regicide, planned by her, is discovered by the nobles, she announces deceitfully "What! in our house?" (*Mac.* 2.3.86). Her politically deceiving behavior continues: When her husband is forced to speak about his motive to kill the chamberlains, she faints, drawing the aristocrats' attention from her husband to her (Cf. *Mac.* 2.3).

The Egyptian queen excels in her "infinite variety" of deceptions and is furthermore a highly political thinking woman. She assumes her opponent's reactions correctly and knows that the marriage between Antony and Octavia was arranged and politically motivated by Caesar. With her unforeseeable actions she secures her reign, making Egypt's enemies fear her (Cf. *Ant.* 2.1.21-22). Although she rules Egypt she presents herself as a woman having affairs with influential Roman rulers. Her immoral behavior damages her reputation in Rome but does not bother her in Egypt. Nevertheless, she gains political advantages through her affairs, e.g., obtaining part of Antony's territory (Cf. *Ant.* 3.6.9-11).

In contrast to Juliet's loyalty to Romeo and Lady Macbeth's loyalty to her husband, Cleopatra seems to be torn between her political considerations for her country and her loyalty to Antony.

5.3 The Author's Impact

Shakespeare wrote the three tragedies presumably in the order as they are presented in this study: Romeo and Juliet in 1595, Macbeth in 1605/1606 and Antony and Cleopatra in 1607. The young Shakespeare depicts Juliet as a less complex character than Lady Macbeth or Cleopatra. Around ten years later, he shows Lady Macbeth as a mature woman character, which stand in contrast to Juliet, and, presumably only around one or two years later, he depicts Cleopatra as a highly controversial female sovereign who is so complex that an absolute characterization of her seems impossible.

Even Shakespeare's dramatic expertise and his stylistic writing skills show a development as far as the depiction of contrasting roles and the character conforming use of language are concerned. The Nurse in *Romeo and Juliet,* Lady Macduff in *Macbeth,* and Octavia in *Antony and Cleopatra* fulfill the function to contrast the female protagonist's characters. Through them, the rebellious nature of the female protagonists with regard to social norms is highlighted. It seems that the distance between the major female characters and their contrasting counterparts increases from *Romeo and Juliet* to *Antony and Cleopatra.*

The Nurse raised Juliet and is presented in direct contact with her. The Nurse's casualness and her practical understanding of marriage is the greatest difference to Juliet's ideal of marriage and her innocent naivety at the beginning of the play.

In contradiction of the Nurse, Lady Macduff never meets her contrasting counterpart. Lady Macduff is Macbeth's and Lady Macbeth's subject and represents the good womanly weakness which stands out against the mighty evil of Macbeth's reign. Whereas Lady Macduff and her children become innocently slaughtered by Macbeth's *male* cruelty (which Lady Macbeth provoked), it is Lady Macbeth's guilty conscience that kills her. Good versus evil and innocence versus guilt are portrayed by their characters. Lady Macbeth and Lady Macduff live in the same country in which the same social rules exist. These are violated by Lady Macbeth and her husband.

In contrast to this, Octavia and Cleopatra are worlds apart. Like Lady Macbeth and Lady Macduff, they never meet in the play and their difference in character is striking. Octavia represents the very opposite of Cleopatra: She is dependent on her brother and obedient to him as well as to her later husband Antony. Cleopatra is not married and presents her independence and sovereignty over Egypt and herself until the end. She is powerful and manages to deceive even Octavius Caesar.

Next to the increase of the distance between the contrasting roles, also the language seems to increase in its variety. Solely the Nurse shows in her speeches in *Romeo and Juliet* a casual slang and the meter of her lines is not always coherent. In *Macbeth*, Lady Macbeth speaks in prose during her sleepwalking scene which shows her insane and unconscious state effectively. In *Antony and Cleopatra,* the meter varies more than in the other two tragedies. Although no prose parts are integrated, the structure of iambic pentameter does not stay coherent.

Furthermore, the female protagonists become not only more independent but also more responsible for their actions. Romeo and Juliet's love is determined by fate: Both characters are looking for love when they first meet each other: Romeo kills Juliet's cousin in rage, the letter to Romeo never arrives etc. Therefore scholars often apply the term "tragedy of fate" for *Romeo and Juliet*. For this reason, the characters are not completely made responsible for their actions but are mainly influenced by fate.

Still, also in *Macbeth* the witches' prophecy can be seen as a foreshadowing of the protagonist's fall. Nevertheless, they do not force Macbeth to commit the regicide. It is Lady Macbeth who chooses to ally with the witches and deny her identity. Although Macbeth is influenced by his wife, his own ambition leads him to perform the immoral deed. In contrast to Romeo and Juliet, Macbeth reflects on his deed later on and his life resembles "a tale / Told by an idiot" (Mac. 5.5.26-27). Even though in her sleep, Lady Macbeth realizes her guilt and impact on the performance of the murder. Despite the fact that witchcraft plays an important part in *Macbeth,* it is not the witches magic who kills the king but a decision by the protagonist and his wife.

In *Antony and Cleopatra* a soothsayer exists as well although he does not seem to influence the characters' decisions. Antony sends him away and neglects his advice to return to Egypt. When Antony eventually decides to return to Cleopatra, which was advised by the soothsayer before, he explains his decision by his want to return to his "pleasure" (Cf. *Ant.* 2.4.39) in Egypt. The soothsayer's advice seems not the major cause for Antony to make this decision. Antony's words after he followed Cleopatra's fleeing ship from the battle show his reflective thinking: "Oh, / I followed that I blush to look upon." (Ant. 3.11.11-12)

Cleopatra, denying Antony's "fate" to be married to Fulvia or Octavia, expects Antony to return to Egypt. And while Cleopatra trusts in his decision, he returns. The audience gets the impression that it lies simply in the characters' self-determined action how the play proceeds. Cleopatra fittingly announces: "My resolution and my hands I'll trust" (*Ant.* 4.15.51) and points with this remark to her own actions. With "her own hands" she determines her fate as well. Her apparently inevitable fate to be presented in Rome as Caesar's symbol for his victory over Egypt she averts by restoring her royal honor as queen of Egypt through her suicide. Through her effective presentation, she destroys Octavius Caesar's plan and stays undefeated. In contrast to Juliet, who dies out of love for Romeo, and Lady Macbeth, who dies out of the despair caused by her enormous guilt, Cleopatra accepts her death as a necessary act to escape her anticipated bad fortune. This increasing responsibility that these female protagonists show for their actions corresponds with the increasing trend in Shakespeare's time from a fate-determined thinking to the philosophy of life that every human being is responsible for his or her actions and can therefore co-determine his or her fate.

The humanistic approach of an equality of partners in marriage was known in the philosophical discussion during Shakespeare's time. Nevertheless, the reality was that the social roles for men and women were fixed and sustained in the 16th and 17th century. Also Shakespeare does not represent the humanistic ideal in his plays. However, the analyzed tragedies show a critical perspective of the equality of partners in marriage. The theme of equality of partners is most strikingly addressed in *Macbeth* and in *Antony and Cleopatra*. Both couples, Macbeth and Lady Macbeth as well as Antony and Cleopatra, suffer from the violation of the expected social roles. Lady Macbeth is doomed after she gives up her womanly nature and calls on the witches help. Her relationship with Macbeth additionally declines into its non-existence after her violation of femininity. In *Antony and Cleopatra,* the suffering of controversial social roles for men and women is depicted more realistically and less mystically than in *Macbeth*. Major insecurities can be observed in the protagonists' characters, e.g., when Antony's manly honor is violated by following Cleopatra's ship fleeing from the battle and when Cleopatra excuses herself for doing so out of *womanly* fear.

In contrast to their violation of roles, a major cause for marriage is shown clearly throughout the tragedies: love. In *Romeo and Juliet* the ideal of marriage combined with innocent love is displayed. The tragic element is the protagonist's imprisonment by their family's feud which leads, next to fate's influence, to their fall and only possible union in death. Also in *Macbeth* and *Antony and Cleopatra*, the love between the protagonists is present, at least in the beginning. However, the protagonists' violation of expected social roles leads to their downfall in the end.

Taking these aspects into account the three tragedies show a concept of marriage which is based on love and includes the established social roles for women (and men) in the Elizabethan society.

6. Conclusion

Despite the controversial portrayal of women characters in Shakespeare's plays, general tendencies from the analyzed tragedies *Romeo and Juliet*, *Macbeth* and *Antony and Cleopatra* can be detected. On the one hand, Shakespeare's female protagonists violate the accepted patterns of contemporary female behavior. On the other hand, the odds they have to face through their rebellion lets their character fall so that every strong, influential women character commits suicide in the end. Shakespeare's plays present through the downfall of these women characters, who are powerful and who are acting unnaturally according to the contemporary conception, the necessity for strict hierarchical civic order. However, the plays' message furthermore is that the essence of marriage should be love and not merely a rational arrangement which was the rule in Elizabethan times. Astonishingly, Shakespeare again stays relevant until our time. Marriage for love is the accepted norm in western civilizations today. However, even if women's rights and influence increased to a large extent until today, Shakespeare's tragedies show an insight in the organization of society and reveal problems with regard to the blurring of the social role of men and women which is still of relevance nowadays. Shakespeare was no reformist, but he did depict tendencies and problematic developments precisely on stage. Whether Shakespeare's ideal of the role of women was like the one displayed by those female characters that conform to the contemporary expectations, or whether he approved of the role of women that the rebellious protagonists present in the tragedies, is questionable. Based on the presentation of the role of women in the analyzed tragedies, merely the themes presented in the tragedies are proof for the author's awareness of the social rules that suppressed women's independence in Shakespeare's time. Juliet, Lady Macbeth and Cleopatra do not only represent human beings of amazing liveliness but in their completion, they stage women of infinite variety.

7. References

Primary literature

The Holy Bible: King James Version; The New Cambridge Paragraph Bible with the Apocrypha. Ed. David Norton. Cambridge: Cambridge University Press, 2005.

Shakespeare, William. *Antony and Cleopatra.* Ed. John Wilders. *The Arden Shakespeare.* Gen. Ed. Richard Proudfoot, Ann Thompson and David Scott Kastan. London: Arden Shakespeare, 1995.

Shakespeare, William. *Macbeth.* Ed. Kenneth Muir. *The Arden Shakespeare.* Gen. Ed. Richard Proudfoot, Ann Thompson and David Scott Kastan. London: Routledge, 1984.

Shakespeare, William. *Romeo and Juliet.* Ed. Brian Gibbons. *The Arden Shakespeare.* Gen. Ed. Richard Proudfoot, Ann Thompson and Scott Kastan. London: Arden Shakespeare, 1980.

Secondary literature

Adelman, Janet. "'Born of Woman': Fantasies of Maternal Power in 'Macbeth.'" *Shakespeare for Students: Critical Interpretations of "As You Like It", "Hamlet", "Julius Caesar", "Macbeth", "The Merchant of Venice", "A Midsummer Night's Dream", "Othello", and "Romeo and Juliet".* Ed. Mark W. Scott. Detroit: Gale, 1992. 285-288.

Barker, Deborah E., and Ivo Kamps, eds. *Shakespeare and Gender: A History.* London: Verso Publ., 1995.

Bernhard Jackson, Gabriele. "Topical Ideology: Witches, Amazons, and Shakespeare's Joan of Arc." *Shakespeare and Gender: A History.* Ed. Deborah E. Barker and Ivo Kamps. London: Verso Publ., 1995. 142-167.

Callaghan, Dympna. *Shakespeare Without Women: Representing Gender and Race on the Renaissance Stage.* London: Routledge, 2000.

Cañadas, Ivan. *Public Theater in Golden Age Madrid and Tudor-Stuart London: Class, Gender and Festive Community.* Aldershot: Ashgate Publishing, 2005.

Coleridge, Samuel Taylor. "Extracts from a report by J. P. Collier of a lecture given by Coleridge (1811-1812)". *Shakespeare's Early Tragedies: "Richard III", "Titus Andronicus" and "Romeo and Juliet"; A Casebook.* Ed. Neil Taylor and Bryan Loughrey. London: Macmillan, 1990. 35-36.

Cook, Judith. *Women in Shakespeare.* London: Harrap, 1980.

Curry, Walter Clyde. "The Demonic Metaphysics of 'Macbeth.'" *Shakespeare for Students: Critical Interpretations of "As You Like It", "Hamlet", "Julius Caesar", "Macbeth", "The Merchant of Venice", "A Midsummer Night's Dream", "Othello", and "Romeo and Juliet".* Ed. Mark W. Scott. Detroit: Gale, 1992. 256-259.

Dash, Irene G. *Wooing, Wedding and Power: Women in Shakespeare's Plays.* New York: Columbia University Press, 1981.

Dusinberre, Juliet. *Shakespeare and the Nature of Women.* London: Macmillan, 1975.

Fielitz, Sonja, ed. *Literature as History/ History as Literature: Fact and Fiction in Medieval to Eighteenth-Century British Literature.* Frankfurt/ Main: Peter Lang, 2007.

Franssen, Paul J. C. "The Life and Opinions of William Shakespeare, Gentleman: Biography between Fact and Fiction." *Literature as History/ History as Literature. Fact and Fiction in Medieval to Eighteenth-Century British Literature.* Ed. Sonja Fielitz. Frankfurt/ Main, Peter Lang: 2007. 63-78.

Griffin, Alice. *Shakespeare's Women in Love.* Raleigh: Pentland, 2001.

Hackett, Helen. *Virgin Mother, Maiden Queen.* London: Macmillan, 1995.

Kahn, Coppélia. *Roman Shakespeare: Warriors, Wounds and Women.* London: Routledge, 1997.

Klein, Jürgen. *Elisabeth I. und ihre Zeit.* München: Beck, 2004.

Leech, Clifford. "The Moral Tragedy of 'Romeo and Juliet.'" *English Renaissance Drama: Essays in Honor of Madeline Doran & Mark Eccles*. Ed. Standish Henning, Robert Kimbrough, and Richard Knowles. Southern Illinois University Press, 1976. 59-75. *Shakespeare for Students: Critical Interpretations of "As You Like It", "Hamlet", "Julius Caesar", "Macbeth", "The Merchant of Venice", "A Midsummer Night's Dream", "Othello", and "Romeo and Juliet"*. Ed. Mark W. Scott. Detroit: Gale, 1992. 506-509.

Levin, Carole. *The Heart and Stomach of a King. Elizabeth I and the Politics of Sex and Power*. Philadelphia: University of Pennsylvania Press, 1994.

Macfarlane, Alan. *Witchcraft in Tudor and Stuart England. A Regional and Comparative Study*. London: Routledge, 1970.

Mahood, M. M. *Wordplay in Romeo and Juliet*. (London: 1957). 56-72. Ed. Taylor, Neil and Loughrey, Bryan, eds. *Shakespeare's Early Tragedies: "Richard III", "Titus Andronicus" and "Romeo and Juliet"; A Casebook*. London: Macmillan, 1990. 152-167.

Märtin, Doris. *Shakespeares 'Fiend-like Queens': Charakterisierung, Kontext und dramatische Funktion der destruktiven Frauenfiguren in „Henry VI", „Richard III", „King Lear" und „Macbeth"*. Heidelberg: Winter, 1992.

The Oxford English Dictionary. 2nd ed. Vol. 17. Oxford: Clarendon, 1989.

Rackin, Phyllis. *Shakespeare and Women*. Oxford: Oxford University Press, 2005.

Rackin, Phyllis. "Engendering the Tragic Audience: The Case of Richard III." *Shakespeare and Gender: A History*. Ed. Deborah E. Barker and Ivo Kamps. London: Verso, 1995. 263-282.

Ramsey, Jarold. "The Perversion of Manliness in 'Macbeth.'" *Shakespeare for Students: Critical Interpretations of "As You Like It", "Hamlet", "Julius Caesar", "Macbeth", "The Merchant of Venice", "A Midsummer Night's Dream", "Othello", and "Romeo and Juliet"*. Ed. Mark W. Scott. Detroit: Gale, 1992. 263-269.

Ribner, Irving. "'Macbeth': The Pattern of Idea and Action." *Shakespeare for Students: Critical Interpretations of "As You Like It", "Hamlet", "Julius Caesar", "Macbeth", "The Merchant of Venice", "A Midsummer Night's Dream", "Othello", and "Romeo and Juliet"*. Ed. Mark W. Scott. Detroit: Gale, 1992. 245-251.

Scott, Mark W., ed. *Shakespeare for Students. Critical Interpretations of "As You Like It", "Hamlet", "Julius Caesar", "Macbeth", "The Merchant of Venice", "A Midsummer Night's Dream", "Othello", and "Romeo and Juliet"*. Detroit: Gale, 1992.

Schoenbaum, Samuel. *William Shakespeare: A Compact Documentary Life*. Oxford: Oxford University Press, 1987.

Schormann, Vanessa. *Macbeth*. Hrsg. Sonja Fielitz. Bochum: Kamp, 2005.

Spender, Stephen. "Books and the War – II." *Shakespeare for Students: Critical Interpretations of "As You Like It", "Hamlet", "Julius Caesar", "Macbeth", "The Merchant of Venice", "A Midsummer Night's Dream", "Othello", and "Romeo and Juliet"*. Ed. Mark W. Scott. Detroit: Gale, 1992. 261-263.

Stevens, Martin. "Juliet's Nurse: Love's Herald." *Papers on Language & Literature, 2.3* (1966): 195-206. Rpt. in *Shakespeare for Students: Critical Interpretations of "As You Like It", "Hamlet", „Julius Caesar", "Macbeth", "The Merchant of Venice", "A Midsummer Night's Dream", "Othello", and "Romeo and Juliet"*. Ed. Mark W. Scott. Detroit: Gale, 1992. 514-519.

Valerius, Robert. *Weibliche Herrschaft im 16. Jahrhundert. Die Regentschaft Elizabeths I. zwischen Realpolitik, Querelle des femmes und Kult der Virgin Queen*. Herbolzheim: Centaurus Verlag, 2002.

Printed in Great Britain
by Amazon

27257496R00040